NORMAN MAILER

MODERN MASTERS

Already published

MODERN MASTERS

EDITED BY frank kermode

norman mailer

richard poirier

NEW YORK | THE VIKING PRESS

Copyright © 1972 by Richard Poirier
All rights reserved
Published in 1972 in a hardbound
and paperbound edition by
The Viking Press, Inc.
625 Madison Avenue, New York, N.Y. 10022
SBN 670-51503-5 (hardbound)
670-01917-8 (paperbound)
Library of Congress catalog card number: 75-185983
Printed in U.S.A.

ACKNOWLEDGMENTS

Little, Brown and Company: From *The Prisoner of Sex*
by Norman Mailer.
Copyright © 1971 by Norman Mailer.
Reprinted by permission of Little, Brown and Co.

Scott Meredith Literary Agency, Inc.:
From *An American Dream* by Norman Mailer.
Copyright © 1964, 1965 by Norman Mailer.
From *Cannibals and Christians* by Norman Mailer.
Copyright © 1966 by Norman Mailer.
Reprinted by permission of the author and
the author's agents, Scott Meredith Literary Agency, Inc.

The New American Library, Inc.:
From *The Armies of the Night* by Norman Mailer.
Copyright © 1968 by Norman Mailer. Reprinted by
arrangement with New American Library, Inc.

G. P. Putnam's Sons:
From *The Deer Park*, Copyright © 1955 by Norman Mailer;
Advertisements For Myself,
Copyright © 1959 by Norman Mailer;
The Presidential Papers, Copyright © 1960, 1961,
1962, 1963 by Norman Mailer;
and *Why Are We in Vietnam?*,
Copyright © 1967 by Norman Mailer.

TO MARTIN DUBERMAN

CONTENTS

A NOTE OF THANKS

> Anita Van Vactor and Thomas Edwards
> were often in mind as ideal readers
> while I wrote this book, and it is
> better than it would have been
> for their advice and inspiration.

BIOGRAPHICAL NOTE

1923   Born January 31, Long Branch, New Jersey, son of Isaac Barnett Mailer (who emigrated from South Africa via London after World War I) and Fanny (Schneider) Mailer.

1927   Family moves to the Eastern Parkway section of Brooklyn.

1939   Enters Harvard to study aeronautical engineering, after schooling at P.S. 161 and Boys' High School, Brooklyn; becomes interested in writing. ("All through December 1939 and January 1940 I was discovering modern American literature.")

1941   Wins *Story* magazine's annual college contest with "The Greatest Thing in the World"; on *Harvard Advocate*, the undergraduate literary magazine; writing stories influenced by Hemingway; writes his first novel (*No Percentage*, about Jewish life in Brooklyn) during the summer (unpublished—"It was just terrible").

1943   Graduates from Harvard, writes an unpublished novel (*A Transit to Narcissus*) based on experiences working at a state hospital in Boston during the summer of 1942.

1944   Novella, "A Calculus at Heaven," printed in Edwin Seaver's *Cross-Section*; marries Beatrice Silverman; inducted into the U. S. Army, serving with the 112th Cavalry out of San Antonio, Texas.

1944–
1946   Overseas for eighteen months in Leyte, Luzon, and with occupation forces in Japan; Field Artillery surveyor, clerk, interpreter of aerial photographs, rifleman, and cook.

1946   Discharged (May); begins *The Naked and the Dead* in the summer, finishing it fifteen months later.

1948   *The Naked and the Dead* published; travels in Europe, studying at the Sorbonne under the GI Bill; meets Jean Malaquais in Paris; returns to United States in time to campaign for the election of Henry Wallace; writes articles for the New York *Post* and delivers speeches on the subject of academic freedom for the National Council of the Arts, Sciences and Professions.

1949   Speaks at the Waldorf Peace Conference; soon after, breaks with the Progressive Party; begins, researches, and drops a novel about labor unions; in Hollywood during the summer, working on an original screenplay for Samuel Goldwyn (who rejects it but offers $15,000 for the "idea," which Mailer refuses to sell); also at work on *Barbary Shore* ("I think it reflected the impact of Hollywood on me in some subterranean fashion"); first child, Susan, born.

1951   *Barbary Shore* published.

1952   Divorced from Beatrice Silverman.

1953   Becomes a contributing editor on *Dissent* (until 1963).

1954   Marries Adele Morales; Rinehart breaks contract on *The Deer Park* over "six not very explicit lines about the sex of an old producer and a call girl"; after being rejected by six publishers, the manuscript is accepted by G. P. Putnam.

1955   Founds *The Village Voice* with Daniel Wolf and Edwin Fancher; *The Deer Park* published.

1956   Writing a column for the *Voice* (January–May); *The Man Who Studied Yoga* published in *New Short Novels*.

1957   Birth of his second daughter, Danielle; "The White Negro" appears in *Dissent.*

1959   *Advertisements for Myself* published; third daughter born, Elizabeth Anne.

1960   Receives a grant from the National Institute of Arts and Letters; attends the Democratic Convention in Los Angeles; "Superman Comes to the Supermarket" appears in *Esquire* three weeks before the election; on November 19, after a party celebrating his intention to run for Mayor of New York on the Existentialist ticket, Mailer stabs his wife, Adele Morales, with a penknife; receives a suspended sentence when she refuses to press charges; under observation in Bellevue hospital for seventeen days.

1962   *Deaths for the Ladies (and Other Disasters)* published; writing a column for *Esquire,* "The Big Bite," 1962–1963; divorced from Adele Morales; marries Lady Jeanne Campbell, daughter of the Duke of Argyll, granddaughter of Lord Beaverbrook; Lady Campbell gives birth to his fourth daughter, Kate.

1963   *The Presidential Papers* published; divorced from Lady Jeanne Campbell; marries an actress, Beverly Bentley.

1964   *An American Dream* appears serially in *Esquire;* birth of his first son, Michael Burks.

1965   *An American Dream* published (revised) as a book; Vietnam Day speech at Berkeley (May 25).

1966   *Cannibals and Christians* published; birth of his second son, Stephen McLeod.

1967   His dramatic adaptation of *The Deer Park* opens at the Theatre de Lys, New York, January 31, closes May 21; *Why Are We in Vietnam?* published; produces, directs, and performs in a film, *Wild 90;* participating in the march on the Pentagon (October 21); arrested and released (October 22) on his own recognizance after being sentenced to thirty days (twenty-five suspended); elected to the National Institute of Arts and Letters.

1968   "The Steps of the Pentagon" appears in *Harper's* (March); covers both political conventions for

Harper's; release of his film *Beyond the Law* (filmed 1967) about detectives and suspects; *The Armies of the Night* published; *Miami and the Siege of Chicago* published.

1969　Receives the National Book Award (Arts and Letters division) and shares the Pulitzer Prize in nonfiction for *The Armies of the Night*; campaigns unsuccessfully in New York mayoral primaries on a secessionist ticket, proposing that New York City be made the fifty-first state; covers the moon shot for *Life*.

1970　After appealing the disorderly conduct conviction (for his part in the 1967 Pentagon demonstration) to the Supreme Court, Mailer serves out the two days remaining in his sentence; publication of *Of a Fire on the Moon*.

1971　*The Prisoner of Sex* published; *Maidstone* (filmed in 1968) opens in New York and is later published in a paperback edition, with an introductory essay by the author; birth of his fifth daughter, Maggie Alexandra, to Carol Stevens; reading performance on December 6 of *D.J.*, play based on *Why Are We in Vietnam?* at a benefit for the People's Coalition for Peace and Justice at Cathedral of St. John the Divine, New York.

NORMAN   MAILER

The Form of a Literary Career

1

One characteristic of the very ambitious writer is that he becomes a theoretician of his own work. In being so, he manages to set the terms for the criticism subsequently written about him. This has been true at least since Sir Philip Sidney, but it has become increasingly the case after Coleridge, Wordsworth, and Shelley; after Joyce's handouts about *Ulysses*; and after Robert Frost pretty much succeeded, through public readings and his loyally repetitious anthologists, in establishing an image of himself that is at odds with some of his best poetry. And of course T. S. Eliot notoriously commanded the way his poetry was to be read (mostly, I think, to its disadvantage), both in the formulas offered in his criticism and in the ruminative language of the poems themselves. For the *Quartets*, there are scarcely any terms available for discussions of the poetry that are larger than the terms used in it.

Criticism has not been conspicuously successful in dealing with this phenomenon. Faced with explanatory language, critics, like most other people, set about gratefully to understand rather than to question it. They do not want to imagine situations, perhaps especially in poetry, where all the words are in motion, where the proffered abstractions or analytical fixtures are as problematic as the material they seem to explain, where nothing is stabilized, nothing a standard by which to measure the mobility of anything else. If few will accept, even fewer will set out to create such fluidity in works where the author has tried to prevent it. To do so is to challenge the sufficiency of the very terms on which the author or the work depends for order and focus. Yet such skepticism seems to me absolutely essential to criticism.

Norman Mailer is a recent and extreme example of a writer who has tried to be the literary historian of his own work, and who in the process has tended to usurp the interpretive, even quite often the evaluative, function of criticism. His self-explanations and assessments are abundant to a fault. He gives so much that one gift is not evidently more important than another, and like an overgenerous lover he finally induces almost a lethargy of gratitude. A man who offers more than anyone wants is in danger of being taken for granted, even of being resented for forestalling what the reader would like to give of himself. Mailer, especially in his most recent work, leads our reading, organizes our impressions, assails us with interpretations of himself that prevent all but the stoutest reader from responding at his own pace, or with free enthusiasm to things that are on the periphery of Mailer's organizational formulas. It is all but impossible to have a peaceful or casual relationship to his writing. Even after the most obedient attention, the reader is seldom rewarded with any sense of achieved calm. The reason may be that Mailer himself is continually agitated and dissatisfied with his achievements, and that he is always redoing his work by his subsequent commentaries on it. Mailer is a writer as yet without the ultimate serenity that is probably needed for the great book he wishes to write. I say this out of the conviction that he is nonetheless the only writer of prominence in English who can be expected to deliver a work that deserves comparison with the best of Faulkner or James. Some of his contemporaries have written more shapely books, almost everyone who might be compared with him has avoided his excesses, but none has displayed his mastery of contemporary English as it has been fashioned not only in literature but in a multitude of media. No one now gives more hope that language may still be the potent instrument of human need in its confrontations with the benign as well as the wicked forces of institutionalized life.

Mailer's writings are best considered as one large work. However thematically repetitious, it is a work which constantly comes alive with extraordinary accumulations of intensity and brilliance. It is nonetheless a chaotic mixture that awaits some larger redemptive effort; so that despite *The Armies of the Night* and *Why Are We in Vietnam?*, Mailer now is like Melville without *Moby Dick*, George Eliot without *Middlemarch*, Mark Twain without *Huckleberry Finn*. The present danger is that he is applying to new issues and circumstances methods that he has already worked to exhaustion and, even more, that his achieved self-explanation has come to precede him to experience. In treating the moonshot, the Ali-Frazier fight, or women's liberation, he seems locked into a system that one hoped he could have transcended.

And yet it is of course Mailer himself who created this hope. By sitting so frequently in self-judgment upon his past he is always implicitly proposing for himself some fresh start in the future. If one gets impatient with his habitual mannerisms—the dualisms and the

mixtures of styles that are meant to catch the contentions at work in the whole culture—part of the reason is
that they represent the souring of what was a fresh start.
The now too familiar methods that portend a crisis in
his career were invented to save him from an earlier,
probably more threatening one. They saved him from
becoming a mere literary writer, one whose acceptance
of the protective cover of moribund literary manners all
but alienated him from the vital changes in his society.
He is still relying on the persona of the perpetually
embattled writer that he began to create in the pieces,
particularly the prefatory comments, collected in *Advertisements for Myself*, in 1959. The degree to which this
persona was invented for literary purposes and the degree
to which it is a necessity of his life is doubtless a mystery even to Mailer. I suspect that without it he would
not have given us the work that followed his first three
books: *The Naked and the Dead*, which was a stunning
success, *Barbary Shore*, and *The Deer Park*, which had
a mixed but comparatively unfavorable reception. What
he would have written, if anything, would have
belonged, as does the last of these novels, to the literary
time of Faulkner, Hemingway, and especially Fitzgerald.

In his sentiments if not in his modes Mailer still
belongs to that time. His cultural conservatism, with its
unmodified opposition to technology and its confidence
in the possibility of small communities or neighborhoods
united organically by shared values, smacks always of
agrarianism. In this as in other respects he is closer to
Faulkner than to Hemingway, who is mentioned more
frequently in his works than any other writer. He has a
Faulknerian mystique about small-town or rural America, which made him a rather curious candidate for
Mayor of the City of New York; he likes to think in
The Prisoner of Sex of the forty-six chromosomes in
each cell of the human body as a "nest of hieroglyph-

ics,"[1] having already told us in *The Armies of the Night* that these hieroglyphics are "so much like primitive writing."[2] The past from which Mailer feels the threat of separation is not Victorian England—that lamentably lamented golden age for Anglophilic academics who have taken an inexpensive but chic purchase on the most readily available of cultural heritages. Rather, he looks to "the marvelous sinews of creation—locked in the amputated past,"[3] which is elusive of any historical location.

He nonetheless finds residual and sporadic evidences of this "amputated past" in certain areas of the present that have not yet been wholly integrated into repressive or coopting systems. Intentionally or not, proponents of so-called high culture, without recognizing that they too are a minority element, provide the standards by which repression and cooption proceed under cover of respectability and the pretense to "standards." Indeed, insofar as Mailer expresses concern for the preservation of cultural monuments (as he does, for example, when talking about architecture), he does so because he sees in them the embodiment of certain human creative qualities that he more frequently discovers in the marginal figures, be they Black, criminal, or psychopathic, whose virtues he celebrates in "The White Negro." Thus he condemns the architecture of modern school buildings because it "maroons children in an endless hallway of the present" and deprives them of a "wound from culture itself." The virtue of the old gladiatorial schoolyard, so far as he is concerned, is that in the very menace of the dark and forbidding building a child might recognize the "buried message of the cruelty and horror which were rooted in the majesties of the past."[4] So too with the

[1] *The Prisoner of Sex*, p. 210.
[2] *The Armies of the Night*, p. 93.
[3] *The Prisoner of Sex*, p. 222.
[4] *The Presidential Papers*, p. 186.

destruction of old railway stations, though the grand pillars of Pennsylvania Station in New York City were still standing when he wrote in 1963 that railway stations in large cities should properly be monumental in acknowledgment of the fact that the act of taking a trip "is a grave hour to some part of the unconscious."[5]

Whether or not these opinions are worth attention in the planning of municipal buildings is fortunately not a question I have to answer. They are important for the moment only in that they help characterize the particular ways in which Mailer chooses to define himself as an embattled cultural hero. Cultural forms or institutions appeal to him insofar as they perpetuate human energies that contemporary life tends otherwise to suppress. Like Emerson, he is less interested in preserving good taste, wisdom, literature, or even learning than in finding, in any form of human activity, some exemplary contention with time, nature, and death. Man has progressively denied the reality of these challenges by the lure of drugs, by which Mailer means any kind of palliative, including verbal ones, and by his technological encroachments on nature.

Mailer, then, is at war with forces so large as to make literary controversy merely one of the battles. "War" is for Mailer not essentially good, but good in the present age where and when it proves essential. Thus while he detested the war in Vietnam from the very beginning for the reason that "all wars were bad that relocated populations (for the root of rich peasant lore was then destroyed)," he can go on to say that there is nonetheless such a thing as a "good war." "A good war, like anything else which is good, offers the possibility that further effort will produce a determinable effect upon chaos, evil, or waste."[6]

Chaos, evil, and waste are three central topics in his

---

[5] *Ibid.*, p. 178.
[6] *The Armies of the Night*, p. 185.

work. And in claiming that a "war" can be good if it encourages any effort to combat them, he is offering us a profoundly important analogy to writing, wherein he makes his own principal contribution to the cause. He is saying that a proper metaphor for the good writing he wants to do is "war." Declaring in 1959 his oft-quoted ambition to initiate "a revolution in the consciousness of our time," he immediately went on "to think it is my present and future work which will have the deepest influence of any work being done by an American novelist in these years."[7] His work would have the effect of a good war. And later, in 1966, he clinched the implication when he defined "form in general"—and this could mean not only the form of a book but also the form of his literary career—as "the record of a war."[8]

To call form "the record of a war" and then to propose almost immediately thereafter that "form is the physical equivalent of memory" is perhaps to take too much license even with the very open form in which the statements occur: a kind of play by Mailer composed of dialogue between himself and a fictitious Interviewer entitled "The Political Economy of Time." Sometimes witty but just as often presumptuous in its efforts to create a Maileresque theology of form, time, soul, and spirit, it would have been better at half its length. But then Mailer would not have been able to display his capacity for modifying his own definitions, to show how in one context it is necessary to discredit a term that was essential to him in another, and, finally, to contrive an argument in which all of the terms end up ingeniously linked to one another. Along with an equally ambitious play-interview, "The Metaphysics of the Belly," and the essay "The White Negro," "The Political Economy of Time" is indispensable to any understand-

---

[7] *Advertisements for Myself*, p. 17.
[8] *Cannibals and Christians*, p. 370.

ing of Mailer's *œuvre*. Taken together the three provide his core terminology and, more importantly, a clue to how certain key terms and ideas move about in his mind and writing. The term "form" in the passage I shall shortly quote, for example, is, like others that are used repeatedly by Mailer, meanderingly in motion. It is as if he gives a certain word the responsibility to absorb and recreate and in turn be enriched by other words that it comes into contact with in a phrase or a sentence; as if he gives it the responsibility of searching out a predictable but as yet unmapped area of larger meaning wherein all his words will pulsate in a dialectical interchange. Dialogue—with its potential challenges, its invitations to varieties of tone, the possible play of one style upon another—offers Mailer an opportunity for verbal pugilism and is thus a particularly apt illustration of Mailer's claim that a literary form, or any form, can be "the record of a war."

Nonetheless, most readers will not find in Mailer's dialogues the clarifying results that can be expected from, say, the critical dialogues of Dryden. Mailer is always in the position, indeed he puts himself there, of being called out on fouls by critics whose notions of clarity refer us back to neoclassical standards of form and thought. While it can be argued that he therefore deserves what he gets, it is perhaps best to find out first what game he thinks he is playing. Otherwise, the chances of getting what Mailer has to offer would be about as slim as have been the chances of getting what Lawrence or Wilhelm Reich or Norman O. Brown have to offer. I mention these others because their style of thinking, and very often of writing, can be compared to Mailer's, and so can the tight-minded and nonresponsive readings they still mostly receive. Before deciding on the standards that Mailer fails to meet as a "thinker," readers might ask if they are adequate to the standards set by his writing in any given case, or even if they can recognize, much less meet, the unique demands he makes on their attention. Originality does not consist, after all, in violating rules; it consists in creating new ones. But it is unfortunate that even at this late date in the history of "close-reading," it is still not granted to the writer of prose that his style might work to contravene rather than confirm our everyday notions of making sense.

And yet it must be admitted that Mailer, more than any of the other writers I have mentioned, does invite annoyance and dissatisfaction. It is easy to understand why many readers, especially those whose defensive pretensions to high culture get expressed in a distaste for mixed modes, do not recognize the extraordinary complexity and generosity of his style. They do not, after all, quite believe that some combination of William and Henry James would write about "white Negroes," or that a man like Rojack in *An American Dream* can be a throwback to Christopher Marlowe and at the same time a figure out of Dashiell Hammett. Perhaps there is no greater evidence of debilitating snobbery and cravenness in treating literature and high culture as something to be salvaged from vulgar contaminations than the fact that many readers with unusual claims to literacy cannot come to terms with a writer who exercises an exquisitely tuned, a nearly precious sensibility while being in open and free contact with everything from pathological, drug-ridden murderers to Mafioso creeps, to prize fighters. Precisely because it is assumed we all know (or do not need to know) about these things, and that in any case they are not mysteries calling for the metaphysical interpretations he makes of them, even admirers of Mailer have become tiresomely insistent that he be more "responsible."

Why, it is inevitably asked, need he be cavalier about such matters as literary form or war or presidential elections? Why need he, on the other hand, be so obsessed with the digestive system or the human procreative process when there already exists such a mass of "authoritative work," as to make poetic excursions an embarrassing reminder of the possible irrelevance of poetry? Even more, doesn't Mailer's way of inquiring into a subject, with his dizzying refusal to fix on any definition of the terms he is using, flout the very possibilities of reasonable discussion within the community of people who share his interests? The charge of irresponsibility has been made most effectively by Irving Howe and others in the pages of *Dissent*, and it is in great part a complaint that Mailer has stepped outside the agreed modes of debate and thereby rejected the conveniences of political and intellectual consensus.

Addressing himself to issues about which there has been a vast accumulation of work done by other people, Mailer masters this material only that he may justify his escape from the more conventional treatments of it. After all, if he is to effect a revolution in our consciousness it will not be by making the merely usual kind of sense. It will be by virtue of a style subversive of the ways certain problems are customarily handled. In this his position is not unlike that of most writers of unusual ambition except that the power of style, of personality moving about on the page, in his case confronts subjects that are notoriously not to be managed by style alone. Writing with the *élan* of Henry James about moonshots and title shots has its risks, and though he calls himself a novelist, the vastly greater part of his writing is not fiction at all. No amount of hocus-pocus about the degree to which history is really the novel and the novel really history can release Mailer from the pressure of his readers' knowing that they are not the same thing, that the material of fiction is altogether more in the writer's control, more subject to the mastery of his style than is material such as one finds in, say, *The Prisoner of Sex*. It is perhaps there that his exercises in verbal and imaginative ingenuity are most offensive, in that they turn out to be efforts less at daring speculation than at evasion. In almost every one of his arguments he reaches a point of serious peril about the relations of the sexes as persons, only then to offer rather dizzy eugenic proposals about the relations of "X" and "Y" chromosomes. And he confounds his triviality in such instances first by admitting it and then by pretending that he will now return to face issues that he knows have been so blurred as to permit him yet other, even more erroneous flights.

Nonetheless, Mailer's style, given the issues he has chosen to write about, often does succeed in creating a kind of counterhistory. When I say that it succeeds I mean for the occasion of the book, and I do not mean that it thereby also succeeds for life. It is, after all, the books that we are reading. I mean to suggest that Mailer's writing is not nearly so dangerous or subversive as his detractors (and his admirers) usually like to imagine. The form by which Mailer tries to accommodate diverse and often contradictory feelings finally takes better care of frightening impulses both in the self and in society than do the essentially repressive forms subscribed to, less critically and often quite unconsciously, by those who charge him with irresponsibility. It is thus important to discover, as the following passage invites us to do, what he means by form and how his idea of it differs from and often violates ideas of form that are invoked in negative criticisms of his work.

INTERVIEWER   Soon they will be reading your book. This book. This is therefore the moment for us to end and book reviewers to begin. So I would ask you—what is form?

MAILER   Did I not explain?

INTERVIEWER   You certainly didn't.

MAILER   My God!

INTERVIEWER   Is it now too late?

MAILER   My God. I could have sworn I explained it a thousand times.

INTERVIEWER   You did, but then you didn't. You see, now I know that form, and shape, and space, and time, and even death, I suppose, each give off their own special taste to every little pickle in the pickle barrel, but no, I could not tell a soul in five easy words just what we mean by form.

MAILER   I must help you. Certainly I must. Here, have a drink. (*Passes ice and glasses*) Maybe we must go back to the driftwood again. (*Scratches his head*) Is that too long a way for you to go back?

INTERVIEWER   Now that I have a drink it is easy.

MAILER   Driftwood is a fine form. It expresses the essence of form.

INTERVIEWER   Why? Why the essence!

MAILER   Because it proclaims the value of what is kept. Form always makes one tacit statement—it says: I am a definite *form* of existence, I choose to have character and quality, I choose to be recognizable, I am—everything considered—the best that could be done under the circumstances, and so superior to a blob.

INTERVIEWER   Bravo!

MAILER   Yes, driftwood is a fine form. It tells us what in a piece of wood proved most dear to the wood, what resisted decomposition the longest, what—if we know how to read it—was saved by accident, what was etched by design. The form of driftwood is the record of a siege.

INTERVIEWER   But driftwood rots from the outside in —which suggests that its center is not so much essential as most protected?

MAILER   What is most valuable is usually most protected. When the center is not valuable, it rots, it rots first. Occasionally we see driftwood which has hollows in its heart or holes. Form in general—now I let you in on the secret—is the record of a war.

INTERVIEWER   Of a war? Damn you! Of a war?

MAILER   It is the record, as seen in a moment of rest; yes, it is the record of a war which has been taking place. Don't you see whatever is alive, or intent, or obsessed, must wage an active war: it creates the possibility for form in its environment by its every attempt to shape the environment. Wherever the environment resists, the result is a form. When the soul is mighty and the environment resists mightily, the form is exceptional or extraordinary. Sometimes it speaks of what is great or exquisite. Stone hoisted up ramps by men became the pyramids. Cut by crude iron tools and harder stone, shaped over years by sculptors who attacked the rock out of the stone of their own being, one had Chartres, Notre Dame. Today the stones are made from liquid cooked in vats and rolled into blocks or sheets. Fiberglas, polyethylene, bakelite, styrene, styronware. The environment has less resistance than a river of milk. And the houses and objects built from these liquids are the record of a strifeless war, a liquidation of possibilities. But forgive me for the diatribe.

INTERVIEWER   Then let me give the emphasis here. You say—finally, now, at the end of the day, you remark: form is the record of a war. Of a good war? Of a bad war? Of a sharp engagement? Or a very dull one? Do I understand you correctly? You are claiming that it is the character of the war which creates the particular style of the form?

MAILER   In all sense of duty I answer: form is the detailed record of an engagement—war reveals the balance of forces, discloses the style of the forces, it hints at the move from potential to the actual.

INTERVIEWER   But what of memory? Does form have no existence in memory?

MAILER   An extraordinary existence in memory. Precisely in memory. You could even claim that memory like history is nothing but the record of all the oppositions in one's life, of cruel oppositions, calm oppositions, ecstatic oppositions—war, peace, and love, hurrah. Memory is the mind's embodiment of form; therefore, memory, like the mind, is invariably more pure than the event. An event consists not only of forces which are opposed to one another but also of forces which have no relation to the event. Whereas memory has a tendency to retain only the oppositions and the context.

INTERVIEWER   Then can't you say that form is the record of a relationship?

MAILER   Now that I've emphasized its warlike properties, I can agree with you—form is the record of a relationship.

INTERVIEWER Is it that part of the past which is carried into the present? Like memory?

MAILER It is what survives the relationship. Form is the physical equivalent of memory.

INTERVIEWER Do you know? This is interesting.

MAILER (*Gloomy again*) Yes, but it encourages me to go back to our more difficult notions.

INTERVIEWER Soul? More soul? (*Throws up his hands*) That bloody fucking word. I've heard it too much today. Every time you use it, it leaves an empty space in me.

MAILER I'm afraid it does. I think the British chose the word so that nobody with blood would ever wish to discuss the subject. They didn't reckon on us poor landless inquirers. Well, we're done. I'm glad it's rounded off.

INTERVIEWER No, we're not done. You've brought up soul again. What is its direct relation to form? Tell me again.

MAILER But as I've just explained, it's the father of form. What did you expect it was?

INTERVIEWER I hoped it would not be the mother.

MAILER Form is the record of every intent of the soul to express itself upon another soul or spirit, its desire to reveal the shape—which is to say the *mystery* of the time it contains in itself. And it is aided or resisted in achieving that shape by every spirit it encounters. You see we did not begin to discuss a thing. All the problem is still there before us. (*Yawns*) Now, I quit. No more questions.[9]

One evident fact about this dialogue is that it is meant to exemplify the ideas of form expressed in it. First of all, the interview is itself "the record of a relationship" between the speakers, a relationship that partakes also of the strife, the argumentative resistance out of which form emerges as if from abrasions. The Inter-

[9] *Cannibals and Christians*, pp. 369–73.

viewer (like the reader) cannot disguise his exasperations at Mailer's elusiveness, but the Interviewer is also made to seem like a rather fussy, rather campy acolyte, and this in turn is Mailer's license for a corrective explanatory repetitiousness, for playing the-great-man-thinking with just a hint of satire. The definition of form emerges not as a static proposition but as something jogged into meaning, now by one, now by another contributory suggestion. Form in Mailer is well enough illustrated by this technique in that it is never, after the first three novels, self-protectively imitative of already existing forms, nor is it ever predetermined by the constituents of an event. Rather, it is what can be recorded, what is left of those constituents after they have been allowed to wear each other down. The form then isn't simply equivalent to relationships, strifes, or "wars." It is the recollection of these, what remains in the memory after the fact. Hence, form is both "the record of a war" and "the physical equivalent of memory."

Here we reach a peculiarity of Mailer's writing that makes him at once so daring and so cautious, so seductive and yet, strangely, so often anticlimactic, so demonstrable in his efforts to excite the reader to some pitch of consciousness equivalent to his own even while he is lapsing into rhythms and movements that can best be called onanistic. Remember that among the many conflicting elements that belong to an event, Mailer is invariably one of them, and that the record of this event, the form of it, becomes itself the object of Mailer's scrutiny, the occasion for still other "wars" and relationships. He treats the self that existed in the past as another soul or spirit with which the present self can contend, and his work is at last a record of his continuous wars among the selves that are Mailer. The Mailer who marched against the Pentagon or went to Miami and Chicago is a figure in books written about those events. And yet those books were written by a Mailer different from the one who marched, a Mailer whose memory gave form to the events that the Mailer who participated in them could not foresee—though his anticipations of the eventual form might well have circumscribed or predetermined what his experiences might or might not have been. Finally there is still a later Mailer who is the inveterate critic of his own work and who chooses to make yet another form, not out of events of the past but out of the books he has written in the past. He is forever looking back on those forms which are his work as if they are equivalent to a past that can be reshaped, reassessed in the present. In that sense the form of his literary career, as he wishes us to see it, is an account of what he can claim survives of himself from the past.

What is importantly missing from these formulas is any self-questioning about the form given to his experience or to an event not after but, as it were, before it happened. This will become a major theme in *Why Are We in Vietnam?* with the implication that persons who have been taken over by the power of machines are so controlled in their responses to one another, to nature, and to the world as to be incapacitated for certain kinds of experience and unable even to remember them. A concern of that novel, and of an earlier essay, "From Surplus Value to the Mass Media," is the media's creation of forms that preclude human intervention and are impervious to human protest. Since these forms invariably shape an experience before Mailer can get to it, encapsulating it, making it audible and visible, he must as a writer compete with them. Thus the emergence of Mailer the Writer at war with technology. While this is scarcely an original stance it can still be a rewarding one. However, what Mailer does not inquire into is the possibility that this idea of himself, this "form" which is the record of a war with technology, may be potentially as limiting and mechanically repetitious as any imposed by technology or the media. He does not ask, that is, about the circumscriptions imposed by his notion of form, the limits it puts upon his capacity to have certain kinds of experiences while forcing upon him a receptivity to others.

B. AMNESIA AND LITERARY AMBITION

The metaphor of "war" is more dominant in Mailer's concept of form than is the metaphor of "record"—hence, the solipsistic claim that "an event consists not only of forces which are opposed to one another but also of forces which have no relation to the event." Left unanswered is the question of who is to distinguish between the forces which comprise an "event" and those which do not. The events to which some but not other forces have a relation can only be determined arbitrarily and on the spot by Mailer's need to believe that the events will prove to be one thing and not another. In effect, the determination of the event is already the determination of the form that the event is going to be given, and this happens even before memory goes to work, with its "tendency to retain only the oppositions and the context," the context being Mailer's mood or spirit at the time of the event.

"War" is so much the prior condition of experience for Mailer that any elements not in opposition are treated as mere contingencies. One often has the feeling that what gets left out of his work is a lot of the ordinary stuff of life which he cannot very easily assign to one side or another of an opposition. There is something even of pathos in one's suspicion that a lot of Mailer gets left out too. The Mailer who feels he is on the outside looking in, or inside only by virtue of his empathic feelings for those elements of society which are repressed, or who is on the "edge"—all these are given abundantly. What is missing from the outset is Mailer the rather ordinary good fellow, the son of nice and loving parents, with a respect for learning that earned him the extra distinction of admission to and graduation from Harvard College.

In Mailer's theory of form as "the record of a war" there is a justification for a kind of amnesia. Indeed, this seems to have been the precondition for his becoming the kind of writer he was determined to become as a boy of sixteen. Not accidentally, the language in which he discusses form hints at the illusion of self-creation. Form, he says, "is what survives a relationship"; form, he says earlier, is "superior to a blob." It is superior, one might say, to "the one personality he found insupportable," as he later reveals in *The Armies of the Night*, "—the nice Jewish boy from Brooklyn" who "had the softness of a man early accustomed to mother love."[10] If "form is the physical equivalent of memory" then Mailer, whose writings are wholly without reminiscence of his life before he became a writer, can be thought of as his own begetter. But I anticipate an argument I shall make later. Now I want simply to account for the form of Mailer's career, and the form of Mailer that he chose to imagine long before he consciously contrived the idea of form as "the record of a war."

What we discover, looking back, is that war has always been his subject. It starts as early as his writings when he was a freshman at Harvard. Listening in September 1939 to a lecture by Archibald MacLeish, he penned the shortest of his stories, called "It":

We were going through the barbed-wire when a machine gun started. I kept walking until I saw my head lying on the ground.
"My God, I'm dead," my head said.
And my body fell over.[11]

[10] *The Armies of the Night*, p. 134.
[11] *Advertisements for Myself*, p. 391.

Three years later he wrote yet another war story, "A Calculus at Heaven." It is astonishingly good for someone of nineteen, still in college, and with as yet no direct experience of Army life or of war. Set in the Pacific, as *The Naked and the Dead* was to be, it is also predictive of the novel in style, form, and incident. It is in the mode of Dos Passos, full of flashbacks to the prewar lives of the various characters, all of them part of the doomed action on an island named Tinde. And each of these recollected lives refers us, again as in *The Naked and the Dead*, to different enclaves of American society. There is an Irish priest named Father Meary, an Italian from Terre Haute named DaLucci, an American Indian named Sergeant Rice, a Jew from New Jersey named Wexler who has also been a college football player at the University of Minnesota. All of these have racial and other similarities to characters in the novel, and Wexler goes on an expedition that is in detail similar to the one undertaken there by Sergeant Martinez. But the important character is Captain Bowen Hilliard, who, as the Wasp son of a regular Army colonel, a graduate of Yale "with the creative clique; surrealist poetry was in vogue,"[12] is much like Lieutenant Hearn in *The Naked and the Dead*. More interesting still, he is in many ways like the Mailer of later years. The Mailer who in 1944 was to tell Edwin Seaver that "I'd like to be another Malraux"[13] had already allowed the hero of this story to jot down a statement about that writer which carries the burden, while showing little of the tautness, that will become familiar.

> He would write; "Malraux says that all that men are willing to die for tends to justify their fate by giving it a foundation in dignity. Perhaps, everywhere, this is felt. But in America, men live, work and die with-

[12] *Ibid.*, p. 35.
[13] *Ibid.*, p. 29.

out even the rudest conception of a dignity. At their death . . . well then they wonder what the odds are on a heaven, and perhaps they make futile desperate bets on it, adding up their crude moral calculus so that if the big team, heaven, comes through and wins and therefore exists, they will be able to collect their bets that evening. . . ."[14]

Hilliard's attitude toward America in 1942 looks forward to Mailer's in the mid-1950s: "He had postulated a something to rail against. And that 'something' had most often been the word America."[15] Predicted here is the Mailer who, when he finds it difficult to get his third novel *The Deer Park* into print, decides that what he had fictionally postulated about America was probably true: it was "in fact a real country which did real things and ugly things to the characters of more people than just the characters in my books."[16] Though a painter, Hilliard has also written, as Mailer is to write, a big book that fails. Entitled *The Artist in Transit Inglorious*, and "published by a wildcat liberal firm, it made him very little money, but it served as meat for more than a few of the family-newspaper critics,"[17] one of whom berates him for writing that "to die in terms of a subsequent humanity is a form of emotional sophistication that may be achieved only by the people of that nation which puts its philosophy in action."[18] Shorn of Mailer's early progressive liberalism, this idea of action was to flower in the definition of hip in 1957 in "The White Negro," and it includes an idea that was to become equally recurrent: that death is an experience of life, perhaps the final orgasm into the future.

In this earliest fiction Mailer is, in effect, creating the future which he is to inhabit and call his career. "A

[14] *Ibid.*, p. 42.
[15] *Ibid.*, p. 64.
[16] *Ibid.*, p. 233.
[17] *Ibid.*, p. 50.
[18] *Ibid.*, p. 65.

Calculus at Heaven" and "It" are evidence that "war" was the determining form of his imagination long before he had the direct experiences of war that went into his first big novel. I suspect that he might have written some close equivalent of that novel without having served as a rifleman with the 112th Cavalry out of San Antonio, Texas, for eighteen months in the Philippines and Japan. So that while he may propose in 1966 that form is "the record of a war" and imply that this idea illumines his past work, it is clear that it is an idea operative from the beginning, for which the formulations in "The Political Economy of Time" constitute the elevation into theory of a lifelong predilection. "War" is the *prior* condition of his experience. It determines the aspects of experience that are to be recorded and, therefore, the form of his books and of his career —which is perhaps why there are only fragments here and there in his writings before the war which refer to adolescent experience, as in the little story of 1941 entitled "Maybe Next Year" with its heavy dependence on Sherwood Anderson. It is as if when he became a writer he had no past he chose to write about, as if to write about a childhood, which on his own testimony was a happy one, would have revealed him as a mere "blob" and rather than do this he preferred to live in an anticipated future—the war in the Pacific and, beyond that, "war" as a way of life.

The form of a literary career, regardless of who invents it, be it the writer, critic, or merely the calendar, is no more than one of the fictions derivative from an *œuvre*. Its very existence depends, as do the orderings of a novel, on assumptions about cause and effect, the assumed nature of beginnings, middles, and ends, on peripeteias of success and failure. Its oscillations of creativity and barrenness are very often defined in sexual and biological metaphors, and its ultimate claims frequently depend on supposed connections between writing as an activity and all sorts of other activities that belong to what can be known of concurrent history. The last of these is especially important in Mailer's case because he so often works in a boundary area where the nature of his involvement in a historical event is conditioned by his expected involvement in a literary one: he will become the "author" of the event in his writing about it.

The form of a literary career is most often inferred from the works that have been written. In Mailer the case is somewhat different. The form of his career appears to have been the cause of what he subsequently produced rather than the product of it. The nature of his initial ambition, and a priori assumptions of what should follow from that ambition, substantially determined the lines of his development. This is doubtless true of other writers with some romantic idea of their calling. In the interest of giving to a literary life a form that is more than mere accumulation or sequence, a writer will sometimes commit himself to intellectual and historical, not to mention social pretensions, which belong to myths about literature and its importance. His resources are committed, that is, before he is even quite sure what they are, so much so that the need to make each subsequent move fit into some vaguely predetermined pattern may not even be congenial to his most native talent. It is possible that the very idea of having a literary career as a poet or a novelist—distinct, to remember a warning of T. S. Eliot's, from being someone who writes poems or novels—deprives a writer of his most promising opportunities. Perhaps Mailer's dream of a great novel would by now be realized had he chosen to write about the Jewish boy blob he disposed of in order to imagine himself as a great writer.

And yet the illusion of social and historical consequence, the fantasy that a writer can change human consciousness in a way that will lead to the redirection of history, can, in a very few cases like Mailer's, generate a rare and invigorating power. It encourages him to "war" upon what others are content to leave alone: the "block universe" of William James, the unitary, solid, consistent, and, in essence if not in incidentals, unchallenged form of life as shaped by various institutions, including literature. In any given case, writings that express this sense of embattlement may have little or no direct effect on historical movement or upon consciousness, at least not practically. The effect is always a good deal less than most historically or politically oriented readings of literature like to suggest. It seems to me a worthy enough function for literature to illustrate how and against what oppositions significant possibilities for the self in contemporary life can be imagined, and one has to be grateful to Mailer for doing this with more appetite and more success, however fitful, than any of his contemporaries. At its best, his writing exemplifies the *kind* of effort that can and needs to be made by anyone who proposes to make more than submissive sense of the world as it now is.

One of the most regrettable facts about literary (and political) thinking since World War I is its submission to rules, to necessities, to contrived responsibilities—in short, its neoclassical rather than romantic inclination. The situation is a most complicated one because the works, particularly by Joyce and Eliot, on which these neoclassical standards have depended seem to me intentionally to have exposed their exhaustion. Without claiming these writers for the romantic tradition, I would still say that the energy at work in Eliot and Joyce was ultimately subversive, even while the literary traditions and cultural monuments on which they expended it were exalted. In patronizing Lawrence they were being resentful of a writer who was comparatively free of that deference to literary and cultural inheritances which they thought necessary to pay.

Mailer is a writer still entrapped within the deferential mode of Eliot and Joyce, and yet he is a particularly perplexing figure because the pose he strikes, both in his writing and as a public personality, seems to suggest a much greater kinship to Lawrence. Behind many objections to his work is the feeling that he is not deferential enough; mine is that he is sometimes too much so. Lawrence is a greater writer because he insisted on the authenticity of his own past as against the claims made upon it and upon him by literary and intellectual pasts. As ambitious as Mailer to change the consciousness of his age, he did not imagine that he could do so by surrendering a uniquely personal to a gregariously public persona.

Lawrence, that is, did not think of a literary career as a way to escape from the past, which is perhaps why he never tried as anxiously as Mailer has, especially in *Advertisements for Myself*, to give his work the shape and drama of history. In Mailer's efforts to make a form out of what otherwise would be a mere accumulation of writings, to turn what he has written into a sequence of intelligible development, he offers an extreme example of that ambition to translate a life into a literary career which is brilliantly described by Edward Said in his "Notes on the Characterization of a Literary Text": "In husbanding his energies to shape his artistic life," Said writes, "the writer accepts the passage of time on his own terms: time is transvalued into a sequence of personal achievements connected by a dynamic of their own. The displacement of empirical time by artistic time is one of the happier results of the displacement of the normal human life by the writing career."[19] Mailer wants to do more even than this: he wishes not only to displace empirical time but to usurp it. He is most exciting as a writer where the illusion of the historical effect of his writing is most pronounced and where the recognition of the limits of his own power, or the power

[19] *Modern Language Notes*, Vol. 85, No. 6, December 1970, p. 777.

of any writer to affect history, is treated as an ultimate challenge.

A combative eagerness that takes him against many a windmill, an acceptance of the chance that the enemy may be within as well as outside himself, a bodily commitment to the contests of life, a willingness to meet the enticements of drugs, drink, and pop culture, a wasteful playfulness and the courage to be a fool half the time if that is the price of being more than that the other half —these are among the ways in which Mailer has successfully challenged an inveterate drift toward alienation from himself and from America. America has always been for him a haunt of specters, a cacophony of voices, in which one could not be a hero without participating in the mystery and madness of power. Indeed, it was impossible even to trace the networks of power without believing that the body politic somehow functioned by connections at least as mysterious as those which held together a unit as strange as Norman Mailer. From the very beginning he saw America as a corporate enterprise controlled by forces that were apparently at odds but secretly—and unknowingly—in alliance. The pattern of relationships in *The Naked and the Dead*, for instance, hints at an implicit conspiracy between the fascist-minded General Cummings, with his faith in rationality, and the murderously irrational Sergeant Croft, with his love for violence and his awesome defiance of the power of nature. Though they never meet, it is suggested that they are mutually responsible for what happens to the "liberal" Lieutenant Hearn who is brought to his death by the sergeant because he has first been psychologically and spiritually unmanned by the general. In this very first book, Mailer imagines a kind of totalitarian alliance that was to be articulated further in *Barbary Shore*, become a repeated concern in *Advertisements for Myself*, and a near obsession in *Of a Fire on the Moon* and *The Prisoner of Sex*, where technological rationality and the contraceptive circumvention of nature are seen as part of the same design.

C. THE RELEASE OF SELVES AND THE DISCOVERY OF TIME

The Naked and the Dead, along with the two books immediately following, *Barbary Shore* and *The Deer Park*, are unlike Mailer's later works in that he had not yet learned how to suggest any possible heroic resistance to the encroaching forces of totalitarianism. His heroes are isolated, ineffectual, with merely a rhetoric of engagement. Far from imagining that there is any kind of minority power working in them or in any social grouping with which they might identify, all he can suggest at the end of *The Naked and the Dead* is that the lower ranks are left with "saving ironies," while the powers above them, especially the inept Major Dalleson, predict the repressive mediocrity that is to govern the postwar world. The picture, political and psychological, is bleak here and in the two novels that follow, possibly because Mailer has not yet imagined a hero with whose violence he can unabashedly identify himself. For that reason it is not the liberal Lieutenant Hearn but rather Sergeant Croft who is the secret and unacknowledged hero of the book—unacknowledged because Mailer's obsession with violence even then lurked, as he admits in "An Impolite Interview" with Paul Krassner (reprinted in *The Presidential Papers*) beneath his ideological jowl-shaking about the failures of liberalism. Not until "The White Negro," some ten years later, did his instinctive taste for violence, for a kind of "war" less inhuman than Sergeant Croft's, less abstract than General Cummings', achieve some approximate articulation. He needed to find a way in which violence could be less an assault upon nature than an attempt to salvage what is precious in it and in ourselves.

Had he not done so, he would have become tiresomely alienated from American society, out of cultural and literary squeamishness. He would have become a closet-Hip. Indeed, an aloof alienation was predicated by the nature of his initial literary ambitions. These reveal a conventional dependence on literature, on literary heroes, on the convention out of the 1930s of the writer as *engagé*. This latter contributed to his addiction to "war" both as a large theme and as a nascent prerequisite of his being able to imagine himself faced with materials more demanding than the merely autobiographical ones with which most other young writers begin. In all, his sense of cultural or political embattlement was sufficiently accommodated within the forms of fiction already in vogue, and these included an intellectually fashionable disenchantment with America. His failure after the enormous success of *The Naked and the Dead* was in some peculiar way rather flattering to Mailer: it seemed as if his literary career was a confirmation of what, on other grounds, he had already found wrong with America. Whining on the dump, hampered, he says, by drugs but perhaps really helped by them in that they aggravated his despondency beyond acceptance, he managed to re-engage himself with American society in a vigorously combative way.

He was sustained through all these difficulties by certain feelings about his country, too often misunderstood in him—and by him—and in other American writers who are similarly critical of American life and society. Most of them are rather madly in love with the United States. There is perhaps no other literature quite so patriotic because none is so damning of the failure of a country to live up to its dreams and expectations. Like others who are aware of the fantastic human resources of which America has failed to make proper use, Mailer has an unquenchable affection for the energy, the wildness, the undeveloped possibility that is part of the American scene even at its shabbiest. "The White Negro" of 1957 was an affirmation of those human resources, and it was at the same time a celebration of

Mailer's capacity to be in touch with them more intimately than he had managed to be as a literary young man full of buddy love in the infantry. Approval or disapproval hardly accounts for the ways of responding to what goes on in America. What matters is the appetite for it, the capacity to suffer in and with it, to experience the revelations it makes about its own nature in ways so generous and so horrifying. Only then can one even claim that in hating America it is really America that one is hating. "The artist feels most alienated," he wrote in 1952, "when he loses the sharp sense of what he is alienated from."[20] Literary form as "the record of a war," which he himself elected to fight after *The Deer Park*, a war upon, rather than a meditation about culture or an imitation of wars already fought by other writers—this is what proved necessary to sharpen a sense of vocation first pacified by earlier success and then dulled by early failures.

Even though Mailer's distaste for the direction of American society in his early works did not take as its measure Anglophilic cultural standards that have glazed some of the most powerfully agitated pages of American literature, it depended nonetheless on American literary standards which, by the mid-1940s, were almost as stultifying. In their merely apparent daring, their claim to a native reality, these standards were a brake upon Mailer's instinctive radicalism, especially when it came to his confused but volatile feelings about the relationship between the dialectics of sex and the dialectics of politics.

Sexuality in Mailer's early novels is wholly an expression of other appetites, and is never allowed enough integrity to modify those appetites significantly. While there are some exhibitions of tenderness toward women in the flashbacks in *The Naked and the Dead*, more so than anywhere else in Mailer's work, the tenderness is

[20] *Advertisements for Myself*, p. 188.

made sentimentally pitiable, in the manner of *Studs Lonigan*. It is a sympton of masculine passivity in a book about different kinds of masculine power, especially in the homosexual struggle for dominance between General Cummings and Lieutenant Hearn. Similarly, the dreary couplings in *Barbary Shore* are an allegorization of political alliances that have failed. The affair of Lannie and Lovett is an example of a failure to heal the postwar fractures in the idealistic left; there is a sporadic need in nearly everyone to make it with Guinevere (for which read American materialism as the betrayal of the true quest for the grail), or to accommodate themselves to the realisms of the right as represented by Hollingsworth.

Sophomorically diagrammatic in its treatment of sex, *Barbary Shore* is even more important as a clue to Mailer's puritanical reading of the sexual act. The act is allegorized because he simply cannot read it, then or now, as having a meaning in and of itself. To do so he would have to accept its legitimacy on grounds simply of pleasure. When he came to *The Deer Park* he apparently meant to promote the homosexuality of Teddy Pope into a symptom of cultural villainy, though the book as we now have it offers no way to imagine how this might have been managed. If one is to believe his essay "The Homosexual Villain," it was Mailer's reading of Donald Webster Cory's *The Homosexual in America* which encouraged him to change the character of Teddy so that he was "no longer the simple object of ridicule." Mailer had discovered "the edges of the rich theme of homosexuality rather than the easy symbolic equation of it to evil."[21]

Who can believe that Mailer could have been so blue-eyed and simple-minded as this in 1954? He was talking about what he knew of life or sex only in literature, and what he felt able to "do" with sex in literature. He was

[21] *Ibid.*, p. 227.

unable, at this point at least, to talk about what he did *not* dare to do with sex in literature. For when it comes to homosexuality or evil it is not Teddy Pope who matters in *The Deer Park*. Rather it is Marion Faye, a truly brilliant portrait of a pimp-homo-hetero-satanic figure of the sort that was increasingly to engage Mailer's imagination. He was added after the first draft because Mailer, as he tells us in the *Paris Review* interview with Steven Marcus, "felt a dark pressure there in the inner horizon of the book."[22] Like Croft, in *The Naked and the Dead*, Faye is the secret center of *The Deer Park*.

In the light of Mailer's subsequent efforts to place such characters at the center, they seem in these early novels to be hostages to a literary fortune that Mailer was lucky to have been denied. Like Hawthorne in a number of ways, he was fortunate in that his being a literary young man forced him to lie, even while he mined his truths without knowing it. The truth was simply that perversity and power interested him far more than those efforts at health which led to limpness or defeat. One example of the latter is the schoolboy refusal of Sergius in *The Deer Park* to accept a movie contract because it might corrupt him. While Mailer came himself to recognize this significant timidity in the characterization of Sergius, there are still residual traces of it even in the admission that "in O'Shaugnessy I had a character who was ambitious, yet in his own way, moral, and with such a character one could travel deep into the paradoxes of the time."[23]

"Ambitious, yet in his own way, moral"—such unusually priggish wording is from a writer who claimed in the same year of 1959, as he looked back past *The Deer Park* to *Barbary Shore*, that "I had no choice but to step into the war of the enormous present."[24] He may have had no choice, but he didn't in fact take the "step,"

[22] *Cannibals and Christians*, p. 212.
[23] *Advertisements for Myself*, p. 243.
[24] *Ibid.*, p. 93.

whatever he then imagined it to be. Liking to think of the novelist as "a general who sends his troops across fields of paper,"[25] Mailer in the first three of his own novels is more like General Cummings, who is unable finally to release the power he has so carefully gathered, who isn't on hand for the climax of the operation, and who "might even have been silly if it were not for the fact that on the island he controlled everything."[26]

Mailer's first three novels are indeed like "islands" under the influence of writers who are capable of only rather simple strategies for the massing of social and political forces: James T. Farrell, John Dos Passos, John Steinbeck, and F. Scott Fitzgerald. He had also read Lawrence, and his misunderstanding of him indicates how, in dealing with social and political power, Mailer uses sex in a merely illustrative way. His misunderstanding continued at least through *Cannibals and Christians* in 1966, when he could still remark with profuse confidence that though *Lady Chatterley's Lover* had taught him in college that sex could have beauty, the book had "nothing to say about the violence which is part of sex."[27] Mailer's difficulty, which is very close to a disability, in bringing together the beauty and tenderness of love with its violence is perhaps what kept him from understanding Lawrence for so long, at least till the warm appreciation he displays in *The Prisoner of Sex*. The somewhat priggish Marxism that colors his treatment of sex only begins to be toned down in the later 1950s. By then, as he was to say most directly in 1959 in "Postscript to the Meaning of Western Defense," he felt that "the next collapse in America may come not from the center of its economy, reading one's direction by the compass of the classical Marxist, but within the superstructure of manners, morals, tastes,

---

[25] *The Prisoner of Sex*, p. 152.
[26] *Ibid.*, p. 85.
[27] *Cannibals and Christians*, p. 198.

fashions, and vogues which shape the search for love for each of us."[28]

This statement signals an important shift of emphasis in Mailer's work after *The Deer Park*: the search for love becomes less a mere symptom of social and political conditions and more a species of political action carried out against them. The desire if not the effective condition for such a change had already begun to show itself in his revisions of *The Deer Park*. It is implicit in his efforts to remove his hitherto rather finicky phrasings when alluding to sexual acts. The novel had been turned down by Rinehart and Company, at the cost of a reluctantly paid advance, and by six other publishers before being taken by G. P. Putnam. Rinehart's ostensible reason was Mailer's refusal to take out some lines describing a kind of sexual practice between Teppis, the old Hollywood producer, and a call girl. In fact the scene is rather brilliantly managed in its original form even while being an example of Mailer's avoidance of sexual explicitness. It was later revised when Mailer, much to the distress of Putnam, decided that "the style of the book was wrong," and his alterations indicate how anxious he was to suppress what he had come to regard as literariness. Following is the original version, as reprinted in *Advertisements for Myself*; Mailer's revisions are indicated in brackets after the relevant words and phrases; his later deletions are indicated in parentheses:

> Tentatively, she reached out a hand to caress [finger] his hair, and at that moment Herman Teppis opened his legs and let Bobby slip [fall] to the floor. At the expression of surprise on her face, he began to laugh. "Just like this, sweetie," ["Don't you worry, sweetie,"] he said, and down he looked at that frightened female mouth, facsimile of all those smiling lips he had seen so ready to be nourished at the fount [to serve at the

thumb] of power, and with a shudder, [and with a cough,] he started to talk. "That's a good girlie, that's a good girlie, that's a good girlie," he said in a mild (lost) little voice, "you're (just) an angel darling, and I like you (and you understand), you're my darling darling, oh that's the ticket," said Teppis.[29]

This is in the style of a fairly good detective story, though someone as good as Dashiell Hammett would not have lapsed into observation so drab and uninventive as "opened his legs," and "frightened female mouth." The changes noted in the passage are of the kind that occupied Mailer for some six months during 1955 and for which he makes the largest possible claims in his prefatory notes of 1959 in *Advertisements for Myself*. By the substitution of the word "finger" he obviously wants something more raunchy than he had gotten from the tender and romantic-magazine connotations of "caress"; so, too, with "fell" for "slipped," though the tough-guy "fell" has suggestions of inadvertent and clumsy violence which are to no point, and "slipped" is better when used of a girl as adept as she proves to be for the task being called for; "thumb" was substituted for "fount" because a friend told Mailer that "fount" had a Victorian heaviness about it. But while "thumb" may correct a fault it doesn't thereby represent an asset, since the size of Teppis's organ is not at issue and since the idea of power as in "thumbs down" or "put the thumb on" someone is of no consequence here. Though "cough" is probably better than "shudder" in removing the implication that Teppis is experiencing an uncommon ecstasy, it is otherwise a flat word, and the other changes do not excite comment at all.

Mailer accomplished far less with his revisions of *The Deer Park* than he still persists in imagining. Here as elsewhere he proposes that the style had been made

[29] *Ibid.*, p. 260.

less derivatively literary. But as a consequence it was only made more plodding, which is rather damning in a novel concerned with the myths and dreams of Hollywood and with the lurid nightmares of political repression during the most active period of Congressional investigations of alleged Communist infiltration. The style of the book lacks the eccentricity and wildness that belongs to the world being evoked. There is too much of Fitzgerald diluted with proletarianisms supposed to fit the personality and background of the narrator; there is far too little of Nathanael West, except in bits of the book dealing with Marion Faye. And strangely enough there is scant evidence of the talent Mailer had shown in *Barbary Shore* for suggesting the possible nightmares in the commonplace.

How, then, can he claim that his revisions radically changed the book in its shape and direction? "I saved the book," he asserts, "from being minor but put a disproportion upon it because my narrator became too interesting."[30] To credit this, one would have to know how abysmally boring Sergius must have been before. As we have him, he is a dreary version of Hemingway's alienated war veteran. There is no passion, no rebellion in his prose or in his character. He has the credentials to be tough—boxing in the service, a try at bullfighting —but he never contends enough for the power around him to prove it, even in the elementary ways these talents would suggest. He is supposed to be an aspiring novelist but is in fact so passive in his imagination as not to be seriously threatened by the glamour of filmland and gets drawn in only by the accident of his associations and his good looks. It is impossible that Sergius could deliver us anything commensurate with the subject, especially as this involves the anguish, claimed but not rendered, of Eitel, a big-time Hollywood director denied his chance to work for refusing to testify before

[30] *Ibid.*, p. 242.

Congressional investigators. When Mailer adapted the novel for the stage, the emphasis shifted from Sergius to Eitel who, in the process, is made into so tortured a character that he dies in the end of a heart attack—presumably brought on by guilt over his betrayals in politics and love. In the novel are ingredients for a major political-social-cultural drama, but Mailer had as yet evolved no way of sufficiently exposing, organizing, or revealing its dimensions.

The fact that the book does promise so much more than he was able to manage is probably the clue to Mailer's obsession with it: it revealed to him the crippling limitations of the form he had up to this point given to his literary career. The material in his book called for the perspectives worked out two years later in "The White Negro," and he would have needed, to pull it off, a narrator who was in every sense hip, at the least a Stephen Rojack of *An American Dream.* For one thing, the novel needed much more sex than he congratulated himself for giving, and which the play manages to supply. And while it probably was improved by the removal of what he denigrates as "poetic prose," it is just as probable that the world he wanted to create required something like the macabre verbal Elizabethanisms of *An American Dream.* Above all *The Deer Park* needed a hero of the criminality, the perversities, and yet the radical consciousness that he hints at not in poor Sergius but, again, in Marion Faye. If, as he claims in *Advertisements for Myself,* "the more my new style succeeded, the more was I writing an implicit portrait of myself as well,"[31] then, I suspect, Mailer is confessing to more than he wishes. Sergius is indeed Mailer at this point: he is stylistically inadequate to his visions.

One clue to the problem at this difficult moment in Mailer's career comes in the concluding paragraph of the book. Sergius, now writing a novel in Mexico, partly

[31] *Ibid.*, p. 238.

remembers, partly invents a dialogue between himself and Eitel, whom he has left to his new success in Hollywood. The passage is a strange blend of literary banalities and anticipations of ideas about time and sex which are to inform all of the later Mailer. It is as if these ideas were trapped within an inadequate and even demeaning style:

"One cannot look for a good time, Sergius," he whispered in his mind to me, thinking of how I first had come to Desert D'Or, "for pleasure must end as love or cruelty"—and almost as an afterthought, he added —"or obligation." In that way, Eitel thought of me, and with a kindly sadness he wondered, "Sergius, what does one ever do with one's life?" asking in the easy friendship of memory, "Are you one of those who know?"

And in the passing fire of his imagination, he made up my answer across the miles and had me say goodbye to him. "For you see," he confessed in his mind, "I have lost the final desire of the artist, the desire which tells us that when all else is lost, when love is lost and adventure, pride of self, and pity, there still remains that world we may create, more real to us, more real to others, than the mummery of what happens, passes, and is gone. So do try, Sergius," he thought, "try for that other world, the real world, where orphans burn orphans and nothing is more difficult to discover than a simple fact. And with the pride of the artist, you must blow against the walls of every power that exists, the small trumpet of your defiance."

It was his speech, and he said it well. But I would have told him that one must invariably look for a good time since a good time is what gives us the strength to try again. For do we not gamble our way to the heart of the mystery against all the power of good manners, good morals, the fear of germs, and the sense of sin? Not to mention the prisons of pain, the wading pools of pleasure, and the public and professional voices of our sentimental land. If there is a God, and sometimes I believe there is one, I'm sure He says, "Go on, my boy, I don't know that I can help you, but we wouldn't want all *those* people to tell you what to do."

There are hours when I would have the arrogance to reply to the Lord Himself, and so I ask, "Would You agree that sex is where philosophy begins?"

But God, who is the oldest of the philosophers, answers in His weary cryptic way, "Rather think of Sex as Time, and Time as the connection of new circuits."

Then for a moment in that cold Irish soul of mine, a glimmer of the joy of the flesh came toward me, rare as the eye of the rarest tear of compassion, and we laughed together after all, because to have heard that sex was time and time the connection of new circuits was a part of the poor odd dialogues which give hope to us noble humans for more than one night.[32]

The ideas here—ignoring for the moment the expression of them—are to work at the very center of Mailer's later and more powerful writing: that "pleasure" cannot be divorced from consequences; that the artist creates a world potentially more real than what "happens"; that "dialogues," even "poor old dialogues," offer a source of human hope for change, for alleviation, for life itself; that time can be saved from the dominations of the Machine by insisting on its human measure as this is discovered in the creative powers of writing and of sex, even in the rhythms of copulation. These ideas are destined for a wild life in the later works. Here, alas, they are given an accent that makes what ought to be rebellion sound more like insubordination in a nursing home: "the poor old dialogues which give hope to us noble humans for more than one night." And over it all is a tone of that platitudinous truth-seeking into which Mailer now and then descends, as to the locker

[32] *The Deer Park*, pp. 374–75.

room for the final jawing of the middle-aged football coach and his favorite quarterback at end of season.

Surely the Mailer who was later to propose himself as a revolutionist of contemporary consciousness (to all you "noble humans" out there) cannot ask us to find his "implicit portrait" in a narrator so undiscriminately banal as to invent Eitel's advice: that "with the pride of the artist, you must blow against the walls of every power that exists, the small trumpet of your defiance." Mailer is a long way here from form as "the record of a war," even further than he was in *Barbary Shore*, about which he could say, again imagining the novelist as a warrior, that he had forced himself "to accept the private heat and fatigue of setting out by myself to cut a track through a new wild."[33] Instead, *The Deer Park* is what Leslie Fiedler reviewed it as being: not a book about sex or Hollywood or politics, but one of "those troublingly circular and cabalistic books about books. The story of a boy who wants to write a book which is really the book we are reading, in which there is a boy who wants to write a book, etc." One could go further and say that like *Barbary Shore*, whose narrator, Lovett, is also a young man writing a book which is to be the book one is reading, this book is in some sense about the stresses of apprenticeship and of carrying out tasks already assigned by older aspirants who failed. If in *The Deer Park* the novelist Sergius accepts the literary advice of the older Eitel, in *Barbary Shore* Lovett is at the end writing a novel set in the future that had been predicted by his mentor, the repentant Stalinist McLeod, a future governed by repressive state capitalism. And he writes, as does Sergius, in obedience to some heritage of faith passed on to him by the older man.

The fate of the heroes of both books, treated with rather elegiac approval, is an image of the fate of Norman Mailer at the time when he wrote them: a writer

[33] *Advertisements for Myself*, p. 93.

entrapped by assumed obligations to a past that has both created and circumscribed his present. Like the heritages bequeathed Lovett and Sergius, Mailer's is a combination of outmoded political and outmoded literary styles. To understand how this could have happened is to appreciate what a burden of literariness Mailer felt obliged to cast off and why he thought the revisions of *The Deer Park*, carried out in obedience to this necessity, meant so much more than they did, more than they could have meant in the absence of any radical change in his political and literary thinking. From the beginning, one must remember, Mailer was a most literary young man whose career as a writer was formed in his imagination before he had imagined anything very much to write about. In the last two months of his sixteenth year, he tells us in *Advertisements for Myself*, "I had formed the desire to be a major writer."[34] The desire was "formed"—one notes how even when he talks casually of himself it is as if *he* were a work of art—principally by his readings of American, a few English, and a few Continental novelists prominent in the 1930s and 1940s.

The dimensions of such a projected career called for long and patient siege, accompanied by some probably sobering encounters with literary politicians. Instead, at twenty-five, he found himself the beneficiary of a blitzkrieg—achieved with *The Naked and the Dead*, the only one of his works which has ever appealed to a mass audience. It was not an intimidating or notably original novel to those familiar with such commendable products of World War I as Dos Passos's *Three Soldiers* or Hemingway's *A Farewell to Arms*. Possibly because of its success he was from the beginning watched more carefully than Faulkner had been. Faulkner's first three novels, *Soldier's Pay*, *Mosquitoes*, and *Sartoris*, are if anything more derivative and literary than are Mailer's first three but his special genius was given a chance to evolve

[34] *Ibid.*, p. 27.

without his having to be told at these early stages that he had already become a failure. *Barbary Shore* and *The Deer Park* were rather gleefully put down. The latter was full of clichés recognizable even to the illiterate; but the former, while structured around the less familiar clichés of the anti-Stalinist left, had the virtue of initiating in an inchoate way that mixture of dialectics, nightmare imagery, and the grotesqueness of urban scenes, sounds, and personalities which anticipates *An American Dream* and *Why Are We in Vietnam?* Indeed, *The Deer Park* is an altogether more cautious book than the one that precedes it. It is as if the pressures in Mailer of what he then needed to say had become so unmanageable, not only after but even because of *Barbary Shore*, that without any new forms to move into he had to huddle even closer than before to the protection of existing conventions.

Mailer's depression after these two novels is invariably ascribed to their reception or to his own recognition of their flaws. It is more pertinent, I think, to wonder if he was not depressed by at last recognizing the peculiar and self-limiting direction that he had given his literary career from the very first. This is not to say that he did not imagine a career of unusual magnitude—quite the reverse. The trouble was that the kind of magnitude properly belonged not to him but to earlier writers of a different time and temperament. The popular success of *The Naked and the Dead* convinced him of the reality of the career he had imagined for himself at sixteen. He then felt it incumbent upon him to continue with the large theme—the fractured politics of the postwar left, the kind of world that would eventuate from it, the mixtures of lust and politics in postwar Hollywood—and to make the sounds of a major novelist, as in the embarrassing grandiloquence at the end of both novels.

Required to act like a major literary power, he had not yet created for himself a distinctive voice or contrived his own ways of moving or shifting, his own personal rhythm or sense of duration and momentum. Above all he had yet to translate his fascination with war as a theme into "war" as a metaphor for novelistic form. It is true that Lovett, the hero-narrator of *Barbary Shore,* is a disabled victim of the war and witness to the machinations and death that result from cold-war plotting in a boardinghouse in Brooklyn; it is also true that Sergius in *The Deer Park* is just out of the Air Force and suffering a minor emotional collapse due to his guilt for dropping napalm on Korean villages. And among the best parts of both novels are the verbal warrings among the male characters, in the fine tradition of similar encounters between General Cummings and Lieutenant Hearn in *The Naked and the Dead.* But "war" in the more important sense in which Mailer wants to propose it in his novels is absent from all these works. Outside the dialogue or debates, the style is without evidence of that pressure and embattlement found in his later works: the thrust, the extemporized inventiveness, the eagerness to assimilate the social power of voices not natively his own and not sanctioned by literary decorums, the desire to accumulate vast stores of information and contradiction within sentences that are braced by his pride in their large tactical swing. Though there are evidences here and there in the early works of Mailer's later capacities, the evidence is not sustained or prolonged until we get to the material from the middle and late 1950s gathered in *Advertisements for Myself.*

The reasons for this are not reducible to formulas, but one of them probably is that Mailer's success lifted him above the struggles that he needed but also feared. If his success denied him the exonerations of youth and young manhood, then oddly enough these are apparently what he had denied himself all along. After all, the exonerations are a kind of booby prize for clumsiness, formlessness, for being as yet only a blob. There is nothing Mailer dreaded—and dreads—more than the image of himself as a merely ordinary young man before young men learned to be hip. Before that, one escaped the destiny of formlessness by being a literary young man in the American tradition of rather tough, anxiously heterosexual novelists of the big scene. During these early years, Mailer as a young man was probably a much older one than he was ever to be again. He tells us in *The Armies of the Night* that "he had been born to a modest family, had been a modest boy, a modest young man, and he hated that, he loved the pride and the arrogance and the confidence and the egocentricity he had acquired over the years."[35] In addition to being one of Mailer's very rare allusions to his family and the years before he fashioned his ambitions to be a major novelist, this admission is closer to the truth, I suspect, than are his attempts to claim in *Advertisements for Myself* that he had been only "hoping that *The Naked and the Dead* would have a modest success, that everyone who read it would think it was extraordinary, but nonetheless the book would not change my life too much. I wished at that time to protect a modest condition. Many of my habits, even the character of my talent depended on my humility."[36]

"Modesty" may have belonged to his familial condition, but there was nothing modest—not ever—about his literary ambition. Whatever humility he might try to claim has to be measured against the largeness of that ambition and of his models. In that sense the humility is still his, and the measure, though different, is even larger: to decipher the secret code of the times we live in and, in the process, to change the tempo and direction of the times. Remember that in "The Political Economy of Time" he asserts that "form always makes one tacit statement—it says: I am a definite *form* of existence. I chose to have character and qualities, I chose to be recognizable, I am—everything considered— the best that could be done under the circumstances, and superior to a blob." But what came back to him from the treatment of *The Deer Park* by publishers and reviewers was the image of a patsy, a comic figure, in danger of becoming a bit like the whining and ineffectual Roth of *The Naked and the Dead* or, even more, like Sam Slovoda in "The Man Who Studied Yoga." In tone, feeling, even in phrasing, Sam is a portrait of what Mailer, in 1952, might have feared in himself.

The success of *The Naked and the Dead* and Mailer's efforts to connect himself to a past that was literary rather than personal were a way of keeping him from becoming like Sam; his failure threatened to renew the possibilities. In the story, Sam is "an overworked writer of continuity who has had, and is still nagged by, larger literary hopes." A liberal by habit, but "without enthusiasms and without cause," a man given to discussions of the betrayal of the cause by the Communist Party in the 1930s and of what he calls the "culture crisis," secretly concerned with problems that will later be defined by the Women's Liberation movement, and that already disturb his household, a dabbler in pornographic movies—he is all these and full besides of what are to become Mailerisms. "It's all schizoid," Sam says. "Modern life is schizoid."[37] Or, speaking of the 1950s, a decade that Mailer claims to detest more than any other, "it's probably like the years after 1905 in Russia,"[38] he remarks, and thus explains his disgust for "the smooth, strifeless world" of most journalism of the period. This last thought comes to him while he is reading an article that makes him "angry and how helpless. 'It is the actions of men and not their sentiments which make history,' he thinks to himself, and smiles wryly."[39] Nearly the same sentence comes from Mailer two years later in "Reisman Reconsidered": "Put another way it is men's actions which make history and not their senti-

37 *Ibid.*, p. 179.
38 *Ibid.*, p. 178.
39 *Ibid.*, p. 163.

ments";[40] and still later, in 1959, in "The Last Advertisement for Myself," he repeats the sentence and
remarks, with maudlin misjudgment of his past and lack
of hope in his future writing, that it was "the best sentence I've ever written."[41]

Sam's contentiousness, along with his itching com-
promises, his desire for heroics and his passivity, his
contempt for the writing going on around him even
while his own vulnerability to it means that "his language is doomed to the fashion of the moment"[42]—all
this suggests, in the discernible parallels that can be
found in Mailer's own career and conduct, how close
Mailer may have come to a posture like Bellow's. Indeed,
the story is in every way the most Bellovian Mailer has
written, similar in mood but not equal in distinction to
Seize the Day. It is therefore especially revealing and
poignant that Sam is allowed to define so nearly the kind
of writer that Mailer was in the process of becoming
even though he denies to himself any such possibility.

> The novelist, thinks Sam, perspiring beneath blan-
> kets, must live in paranoia and seek to be one with
> the world; he must be terrified of experience and hun-
> gry for it; he must think himself nothing and believe
> he is superior to all. The feminine in his nature cries
> for proof he is a man; he dreams of power and is
> without capacity to gain it; he loves himself above all
> and therefore despises all that he is.[43]

Mailer was to complain that the success of *The
Naked and the Dead* "had been a lobotomy of my past,"
and to say that "if the past had become empty as a
theme, was I to write about Brooklyn streets, or my
mother or father?"[44] The question might better have
been asked when he was sixteen. He had never bothered

[40] *Ibid.*, p. 98.
[41] *Ibid.*, p. 477.
[42] *Ibid.*, p. 159.
[43] *Ibid.*, p. 184.
[44] *Ibid.*, p. 93.

with the local, the familial, the adolescent theme, with that "modest condition" which he claimed he wanted to protect except as a constant reminder to himself of what he did not want to become. Long before *Barbary Shore* the future was his theme, and in a way it always has been. Even "The Man Who Studied Yoga" is a kind of exorcism of the future he still, with trepidation, imagined for himself in 1952. In 1970, the end of *Of a Fire on the Moon* is a projection of himself and of the reader into some still later time when the very style of the book he is writing, along with a whole career of insistence on certain moral and spiritual values, will seem hopelessly outmoded, will be looked back upon from the vantage point of a technologically dominated culture and judged a curiosity even within that larger dispensable antiquity that is literature itself.

Mailer had to find a literary form in which he could "war" upon himself, so to speak, from a similar but not so antagonistic vantage point of the future. The italicized prefatory notes that make up a considerable portion of *Advertisements for Myself* represent the attainment of such a future from which he looks back with critical perspective on the past performances gathered together in the book. More interesting still is the operation of the future perfect, the "I shall have written" in works of reportage like *The Armies of the Night* and *Miami and the Siege of Chicago*, or the political reporting in *The Presidential Papers* and *Cannibals and Christians*. One reason that Mailer is a great journalist is that he manages to be a witness of the present as if it were already the past. He experiences it from the perspective of his future talk and writing about it. He witnesses the present, to borrow an image from Marshall McLuhan, like a man seeing what is around him only through the rear-view mirror of a fast-moving car. This has become for him a workable solution to problems of time which, in their literary and psychological ramifications, had otherwise proved debilitating.

From the beginning Mailer had that "historic sense," to recall Eliot, "which I may call nearly indispensable to nearly anyone who would continue to be a poet beyond his twenty-fifth year." But Eliot was not thinking of the kind of "past" on which Mailer chose to depend. Mailer's avoidance of the personal past as a subject is so evidently motivated by a desire for historic and literary self-enlargement as to constitute the reverse of the kind of restraint Eliot had in mind. The "historic sense" is in Mailer's case less a deep feeling about a locatable past than a sense of those public occasions or current issues which might in the future constitute an important element of the past. Insofar as the past is alive in his early writing, it exists in the influence of other writers large enough in their claims and near enough in time to induce the illusion in Mailer that he could capture the world around him by looking at it through the gridiron of literature. He assessed even the greatest historical events in terms of their potential literary value. Two days after the Japanese attack on Pearl Harbor on December 7, 1941, while other young men considered their own and their country's future rather than the future of letters, Mailer was wondering, he later tells us with understandable self-amusement, "whether it would be more likely that a great war novel would be written about Europe or the Pacific." His preference for the latter was dictated not by politics, and surely not by comforts, but because "to try a major novel about the last war in Europe without a sense of the past is to fail in the worst way, as was shown by [Irwin Shaw's] *The Young Lions*."[45] Literary strategies preceded him to experience, just as war stories at Harvard preceded him to the real war he was sent to in the Pacific.

Understandably, the literature at work in him was not likely to have been written by Henry James (who is

45 *Ibid.*, p. 28.

at moments strongly felt in his later writings, especially the literary criticism), or by Mark Twain. Rather there was the Farrell of *Studs Lonigan*, notably in the characterizations of such slum boys as Gallagher in *The Naked and the Dead*; Dos Passos, whose techniques for flashbacks contributed heavily to the Time Machine bits in the same novel and to the use of chorus; Steinbeck, who probably suggested in such works as *In Dubious Battle* some of the interplay between biology and politics, along with consequent ambiguities in loyalty among men joined in a common enterprise. And there are touches of others: of Fitzgerald, who becomes most evident in *The Deer Park*; of Nathanael West; and of Hemingway, a strong influence on Mailer's sense of the writer-as-public-personality but less a stylistic one than he likes to suggest. Nor are his claimed early attachments to Lawrence and Forster primarily literary.

But his citation of them and the fact that he has written more literary criticism than any of his novelistic and journalistic contemporaries, except possibly Gore Vidal, are indications of deep and totally serious involvement in literature as an institution. All those writers who initially impressed upon him the glamour and importance of the literary life have at least one thing in common: their books are unusually large in dimension, they maneuver massive social or political or cultural groupings into confrontations with one another, and they are, as a result, rather schematic in the organizations of their material. Materials are assembled and proportioned, that is, within a skeletal arrangement of forces, lines, vectors by which personal relations are raised to the level of dialectical opposition. In the hands of Dos Passos or Malraux, the novel thereby takes on the characteristics of a huge military operation, which is one further reason for the appeal of those novelists to a writer who was to say of James Jones's *From Here to Eternity* (the very title of which is almost disconcertingly ambitious) that "of all the novels I've read by writers of my generation, no other book gave me as much emotion."[46]

Only when Mailer's commitment to literary fashions threatened to stifle his instinctive but still unexercised feelings for war—not as a subject and not even as a metaphor for literary maneuvers but as a psychological, social, and existential condition—did he find it necessary to invent a more invigorating pest for himself than a past made up of the works of other men. As created in *Advertisements for Myself*, that past is still composed of literature and, to some extent, of war. In the prefatory notes, however, both are transposed into a species of cultural conflict and of conflict within the self. The past he constructs consists of his literary career up to that point as seen within the reimagined context of literary and social antagonisms. No other writer of comparable importance has made quite so much out of his own real or imagined bad luck. Indeed, it may be that the most prodigiously invented and executed of Mailer's works is the form he has managed to give to his own literary career. In making that career into "the record of a war" the fact that he exaggerates the bad treatment he received or that he overvalues his early work, especially *The Deer Park*, matters altogether less than does the demonstrated power and ingenuity by which he saves himself and his career for far better accomplishments.

Mailer lost his voice by the discovery, after three novels, that he really did not have one. Out of this condition—which usually dissuades would-be writers and silences many who have written—he then made his literary fortune. His writing began to take form from the very instability of his voice, which means the instability of the self as well; it took its form from a species of debate or dialogue or "war" among the possible and competing voices that were alive within him. Not having fashioned *a* self, not having become *a* man by the

---

[46] *Ibid.*, p. 155.

usual process of accumulation, selection, and disposal of personal experiences, but having instead displaced the self by a mostly learned literary manner, he had the personal courage and fortitude, when this project failed, to release all the trapped, unfinished, stunted, disorganized selves that remained alive in him; and he did so, wisely in his particular case, without the help of a psychoanalyst to sort them out, put them in order, kill some in order to feed others. His mature style supports the claim, made in *The Armies of the Night*, that "he carried different ages within him like different models of his experience: parts of him were eighty-one years old, fifty-seven, forty-eight, thirty-six, nineteen, etcetera."[47] He is accounting for a moment in a conversation with Mitch Goodman in which his tone "went back abruptly from fifty-seven to thirty-six," a small incidence of the shifts in style, especially when he is attitudinizing about sex or technology, by which the sage gives way momentarily to the excited, the fascinated, or the merely tricky boy.

When he remarked in the *Paris Review* interview that he had learned most, technically, from E. M. Forster, he really meant that he had learned something about the possible versions of a given personality. Forster apparently helped confirm his inclination not to think any longer of any personality, including his own, as if it were of a piece. Reading *The Longest Journey* taught him that "personality was more fluid, more dramatic and startling, more inexact than I thought. I was brought up on the idea that when you wrote a novel you tried to build a character who could be handled and walked around like a piece of sculpture."[48] This lesson is at least as moral as it is technical, especially when he connects it with the realization that "a novel written in the third person was now impossible for me for many

---

[47] *The Armies of the Night*, p. 9.
[48] *Cannibals and Christians*, p. 209.

years."[49] As a matter of fact it never did prove possible, except in his first novel, in parts of *The Deer Park* which lapse from first to third person, and in some of his journalism, where he invents third-person equivalents to "I." Mailer is himself aware of the reasons for this difficulty: "In some funny way Forster gave my notion of personality a sufficient shock that I could not manage to write in the third person. Forster, after all, had a developed view of the world. I did not. I think I must have felt at that time as if I would never be able to write in the third person until I developed a coherent view of the world. I don't know that I've been able to altogether."[50]

Before *Advertisements for Myself* the effort to summon up "a coherent view of the world" was made at the expense of those elements in him which apparently disrupted or confused his sense of high literary mission, specifically that personal past he associated with being a "nice" Jewish boy from Brooklyn. In *The Naked and the Dead*, his only way of handling analogous material belonging to his characters is through the mechanics of the Time Machine, through flashbacks tangential to the ongoing action and often tediously disruptive of it; in *Barbary Shore* he circumvents the problem by making his hero-narrator an amnesiac; in *The Deer Park* he is an orphan.

Mailer's difficulty in locating a developed view of the world is essentially a difficulty in locating a self, and while this is not necessarily a problem of literary technique it becomes one as soon as Mailer, or any writer, tries to give his identity to the narrative voice or the point of view in any particular work. Mailer's special distinction, as his comments on Forster will attest, is that he sets out to "confuse" problems of literary technique with personal problems of life. This "confusion"

---

[49] *Loc. cit.*
[50] *Loc. cit.*

is responsible for much of his diversity of effect, his capacity to appropriate the styles of others, first to learn and then to teach the reader what is most inward about them. These are the gratifying consequences to be found in his writings after about 1957, the time of "The White Negro."

Mailer's peculiar brand of existentialism finds its meaning within the personal-literary problem I am describing, and it should be investigated, it seems to me, not as an idea so much as a way of coping with a complex of personal-literary problems. It was a desperate effort at personal salvation, a way of situating himself and his career vitally in the passage of time. The simultaneities of past, present, and future that his brand of existentialism proposes are essentially a convenience to him in his writing, not an idea that his writing sufficiently explores or defends. The convenience is that he is able to coordinate the different aspects or "ages" of himself without feeling it necessary to reconstitute any one of them. His economies, omissions, even blind spots, are made to seem like philosophical choices rather than merely arbitrary ones, and the advantage, especially to his reportage, is enormous. With this in mind we can better grasp the importance for him of a formula already noted in "The Political Economy of Time." Having said that "form is the physical equivalent of memory," he goes on to make a distinction between memory and an event: "An event consists not only of forces which are opposed to one another but also of forces which have no relation to the event. Whereas memory has a tendency to retain only the opposition and the context." Under this dispensation, there is no obligation to the past except as one chooses to reconstruct it. The past is that part of the self that one recognizes in the present as belonging to a dimension of time other than the future. Meanwhile yet another self is being formed in the present, but this self will not be recognizable until the present has also become the past, until the self has moved on to a future and decided again to discover what has survived of its past. Form, that is, is the destiny that awaits any present event or experience.

The process has still further complications. The very act in time of creating form, even of a sentence, runs the gamut of oppositions and circumstances. In the creation of a form, that is, one encounters not merely the self who acted in the past but the self who *is* acting at the typewriter. And then? The completed form awaits a future when it is to be reassessed in yet another form which is self-criticism. It is no wonder that Mailer's favorite image of form is a spiral.

Within the involutions, and the evolutions, I am describing, there is some room even for the Mailer he had learned to distrust—the blob, the nice boy, the modest fellow—room, too, for the literary young man of the first three novels. What is overlooked in the inevitable discussion of the alleged ego-tripping in Mailer's writing is that these more "modest" selves are often at work in the sounds and turns of his sentences—questioning the assertive, the heroic, the outrageous self. Modest Mailer emerges from the style as a rather shrewd, sometimes bewildered, charming, often ineffectual, and even downright clumsy fellow. It would of course be a sucker's game to think that this is the real Mailer, more sincere and more true than the manic egocentrist. Each is an agent for the effective pose of the other, and in fact the stylistic gestures of modesty and recantation are possibly the most calculated of all. They get Mailer off the hook for propositions he makes but wants, in a pinch, to rescind or modify. He is like a lawyer determined that his listeners entertain possibilities even if they are to be ruled out of order.

One example, worth noting because so often quoted, is his admission at age thirty-six, with the first three novels behind him, that "the sour truth is that I am imprisoned with a perception which will settle for nothing less than making a revolution in the consciousness of our time."[51] Quite a claim; quite a hedge. Who is doing what to whom in these odd and devious phrasings? Note that he does not say here that he "has" a perception—something one controls—any more than he "had" a desire to be a major writer. He had rather "formed" a desire, as if it were the result of some aggregate of forces with a life of its own, just as he is now "imprisoned with" this perception, as if it were forced upon him. Furthermore, it is not Mailer the prisoner but the "perception" itself "which will settle for nothing less than making a revolution in the consciousness of our time." Not "the" time, you will notice, which would suggest that the time was something of an antagonist, something from which he is alienated, but "our time," something Mailer shares with ordinary folk who are to have their consciousness changed. He, as much as the reader, is problematically the beneficiary of the "revolution" being proposed.

This is not the style of God the Father so much as of God the Son moderated into a man. Christ was of course the classic amnesiac when it came to his Jewish mother and father: little Jesus lecturing to the Scribes and Pharisees who greets his worried parents with a disconcerting question, "How is it that ye sought me? Wist ye not that I must be about my Father's business?" (Luke 2, 49). Christ was not talking about carpentry and he did not imagine that the business was to be without pain. The destiny Mailer the man imagines for Mailer the writer is a very great one but it is also, for the man, a "sour truth." Like an agent of historical necessity he admits that "whether rightly or wrongly, it was then obvious that I would have the deepest influence of any work being done by an American novelist in these years." Any understanding of Mailer, of the *status* of his ideas in his own mind or in the reader's or in their relation to history, depends on knowing how to

[51] *Advertisements for Myself*, p. 17.

hear such an interplay of voices in any of his sentences. Even while projecting the self of the writer as author of a kind of new testament, he allows, in the angular way the claim is made, for the presence of another, more ordinary self: a resident of Brooklyn and of Province-town, Massachusetts; son of Isaac and Fanny Schneider Mailer; graduate of Harvard Class of 1943, where he learned to dress rather conservatively; a rifleman in the U. S. Infantry who ended his service as a cook (like the hero of the revealing and beautifully fashioned story "The Language of Men"); married four times, so far; and father, so far, of two sons and five daughters.

With the pieces in *Advertisements for Myself*, Mailer succeeded in finally getting his selves into a form. He thereby made Mailer the boy, the man, the actor, the writer into a unique fictional dramatization of the selves at war within him and with those forces without, to which, by the very nature of his diverse existence, he is so acutely vulnerable. He was able to acknowledge in practice that not only his books but also his sense of a self and of his literary career were all a species of fiction. Even more, he could now grant himself the needed license for exploring extreme states of being by giving requisite attention to the mundane ones.

Thereby he proposed to test the consequences of act-ing less as the victim than as the appropriator of the world around him. By conceiving of his work not as a comment on contemporary life but as an aggrandize-ment of it, his literary posture recalls, oddly enough, as from that much earlier time when writing was con-strued less as a career than as a vocation. He would have us believe that he has found the way to let the world speak through him on his own terms.

He can thus claim a kind of impersonality even about his own hangups while maintaining that he writes out of loyalty to calls from the deep. That is why he can prove, on inspection, so elusive at the very points where he seems most assertive—as in his statement about changing the consciousness of his time or in his talk, say, about scatology. He proposes in the latter instance that "the obsession of many of us with scatology is attached to a disrupted communication within us, within our bodies."[52] Mailer's interest in "shit," that is, is represented as a dispassioned, scholarly one; he is prompted by "the obsession of many of us" with it and by the desire to know what this obsession suggests about the disharmonies of bodily and psychic systems. Similarly, in *The Prisoner of Sex* he maneuvers in such a way that obnoxious attitudes toward women and ridiculous standards of adult sexuality are continually phased out into larger concerns about the domination of sexual practices by twentieth-century technology.

Mailer's mutations of style as he conducts an argument suggest that no single voice is authoritative enough, no position he might take flexible enough to include the various nuances, the forces, the trapped but potent feelings that, for him, adhere to any given topic, to any given word. Even his apparent taste for violence derives in large part from his conviction that only violence can release powers, release potentially meaningful sounds otherwise entrapped within systematic modes of argument or thought. To treat his writing as a series of opinions on subjects makes no more sense than to treat one of Sugar Ray Robinson's dazzling performances as if it were adequately summarized in a KO. There is a difference, of course, in that words are not punches, however punishing they can sometimes prove. They belong to history, and they have a history not wholly in the control of the person who uses them. Nonetheless, writers like Mailer can try to get control of them, and the historical reverberations of the writing in a case like his are to be measured by the relative, if necessarily temporary, success of the effort. Mailer never claims that the success can be more than temporary or tentative. What after all

[52] *Cannibals and Christians*, p. 281.

is literature but the passage of time in words? The time through which words pass is measured both by the history outside the sentences and the tempo of history in the sentences. Writing is a way of creating the time of one's time.

The Form of History

● ●

11

Mailer is an unusually repetitious writer. Nearly all writers of any lasting interest are repetitious. The same topics or terms recur in their works with obsessive frequency—think in fiction of Henry James or Lawrence, in poetry of Yeats or Stevens—as if they were compelled to explore the furthest ramifications of their verbal or ideological allegiances, as if it were a matter almost of personal salvation that these allegiances should be exposed repeatedly to the pressure of new and different circumstances. Not for them the merely apparent variety of writers whose interests are dictated by the fashions of topicality, or who are always open to the blandishments of new ideas. It may seem contradictory to distinguish Mailer from such writers of fashion, especially since I have been praising him for being so open to external forces and so willing, in the interests of learning about himself and the world around him, to be a "swinger." But it is very much to the point that he inveterately translates the journalistic issues or events of the day into metaphors that have long since dominated his mind and his work: technology, fascism, dialectics, apocalypse, Being, cancer, obscenity, dread, existentialism, drugs, violence, totalitarianism, waste, orgy, God and the Devil, paranoia, revolution, sex and time.

At some point, any subject in Mailer manages to get linked metaphorically to one or another of these terms which are of course complexly linked among themselves. This is one reason why he is best read as the author of a large work in progress. To make a structural and not qualitative comparison, each of his works bears a relation to the whole of his *œuvre* like that of an act to a play of Shakespeare's. In Shakespeare the terms set initially, very often in the first scene, invariably turn up at the end accumulated, enriched, transformed but still there to make us feel—as if by some steady drumming of sound—that the career of the words has been the heartbeat of the play, that as they issue from the trials and circumstances which they have helped call forth, they are a measure of destiny in the play and of the fate of its heroes. While there is a later as distinguished from an early style in Mailer, just assuredly as there is in James, both can be traced back to some generative mix of obsessive terms and metaphors. What usually happens is that a writer as studious of his own work as Mailer has always been becomes at last able to read himself, to make, as it were, a recipe of what has been heretofore partly an experiment with the words he seems to care for most, partly the accidents of genius and good taste, partly subterfuge. He discovers that, like other young writers, he withheld by instinct some of his most precious possibilities for fear of expending them too soon, for fear of not being able properly to manage or defend them.

Advertisements for Myself is a turning point in Mailer's career: being a remarkable literary critic, he was able there to expose the previously submerged, often disguised, and only tentatively operative forces that had been at work in him. In the process of this exposure he revealed how weirdly loyal he was, up to that point, to "fiction" and to "the novel," to literary form—which was not, as in *The Armies of the Night*, to be confused with the form of history. Indeed, fiction and the novel were what protected him from history. The prefatory matter in *Advertisements for Myself* reveals that in 1959 he was at last ready to take responsibility in historical time for attitudes that he had defensively consigned before then to literary time only. What is most remarkable is that as his terms and evocations moved from primarily fictional modes into historical and journalistic ones they did not become, as one would normally expect, temporized in the process. They did not become less extravagant or any more accommodated to the doggedly presumed aura of rationality which surrounds the conduct of public life and of private life carried on in public. Instead, as he shifted from the predominantly fictional context of the early work to the predominantly historical reportage of the period from 1954 to the present, Mailer became more rather than less melodramatic, more hyperbolic. The discovery in reality of fictions he had once assigned to the novelistic imagination made Mailer into that sort of dramatist whose language is designed to put us in touch with what Peter Brooks has identified as the "moral occult."

> The melodramatic imagination is, then, perhaps a way of perceiving and imagining the spiritual in a world where there is no longer any clear idea of the sacred, no generally accepted societal moral imperatives, where the body of the ethical has become a sort of *deus absconditus* which must be sought for, posited, brought into man's existence through exercise of the spiritualist imagination. Balzac's and James' melo-

drama, and the development of the melodramatic mode from, say, Samuel Richardson to Norman Mailer, is perhaps first of all a desperate effort to renew contact with the sacred *through* the representation of fallen reality, to insist that behind reality, hidden by it yet indicated within it, there is a realm where large moral forces are operative, where large choices of ways of being must be made. I have called this realm the moral occult: it is occult in a world where there is no clear system of sacred myth, no unity of belief, no accepted metaphorical chain leading from the phenomenal to the spiritual, only a fragmented society and fragments of myths. Yet the most Promethean of modern writers insist that this realm does exist, and write their fictions to make it exist, to show its primacy in life. . . . The melodramatic mode of utterance is a victory over the repression and censorship of the social reality principle, a release of psychic energy by the articulation of the unsayable. One might say that the gothic quest for renewed contact with the numinus, the supernatural, the occult forces in the universe, leads into the moral self.[1]

We face in Mailer the peculiar, I think unique, example of a writer who came to discover that his sense of the "moral occult," however much it exercised itself in early novels like *Barbary Shore*, could find its proper articulation not in the forms of the novel or of the literary career of the novelist, but rather in the form of history and the career of journalism—a journalism which gives to that kind of writing an exaltation it has never before received. A hint of this development is offered in his confession in 1959 that during 1954, when *The Deer Park* was making the rounds of publishing houses, "I felt something shift to murder in me. I finally had the simple sense to understand that if I wanted my work to travel further than others, the life of my talent depended on fighting a little more, and looking for help a little

---

[1] Peter Brooks, "The Melodramatic Imagination," *Partisan Review*, no. 2, 1972, pp. 209–211 *passim*.

less. . . . I was in the act of learning . . . that my fine America which I had been at pains to criticize for so many years was in fact a real country which did real things and ugly things to the characters of more people than just the characters in my books."[2]

What can this sentence mean? What is one to make of so scrupulous a phrase as "been at pains to criticize" when in fact *Barbary Shore* is a melodramatic rendition of alienation and, in its projected vision of the future for America, proposes something like an underground, even insurgent career for its hero? The phrase "my fine America" has the tone of fragile sulkiness, as from a lover spurned because what he meant for teasing had been taken for truth. Leaving tone aside, however, if Mailer had in fact "been at pains to criticize" America for many years, how can he claim that he is only now "learning" that his country is capable of doing "real things and ugly things" to real people? Can he mean that the country as presented in his novels was somehow unreal and that fiction is not a form which creates or even reflects reality? If at nineteen he could imagine Bowen Hilliard in "A Calculus at Heaven" as a man faced, as he was later to be himself, with artistic failure, and if he also imagined at that time that Hilliard postulated something to rail against which turned out to be "the word America," what, then, is Mailer doing in his imagination at thirty-two that is significantly different?

There is, of course, a classroom answer to these questions. Fiction, we all know, is not to be confused with historical commentary; what a character is made to say, especially when, as in Hilliard's case, it has the ring of fashionable and self-serving disenchantment, is not to be ascribed to the author even when he is later to say much the same thing in his own voice. So we are perhaps to let the matter stand there—with the proposition that there is a historical world of difference between

[2] *Advertisements for Myself*, pp. 234, 233.

Mailer's early criticisms of America derived from literary sources like Farrell and Dos Passos and the later ones presumably validated by personal and national experience.

One observes such critical strictures not absolutely, however, but in order to be more keenly aware of the circumstances that render them inapplicable. The recurrence in Mailer's later works of topics and metaphors found in his early novels requires more consideration than is allowed by the mere assignment of them to discrete categories of fiction or history, to voice as it emanates from a fictional character as against voice as it comes from Mailer. Who, for one thing, *is* Mailer at any given moment if not a species of fictional invention?

Just as surely as each of us is finally not *a* person but a composite of a number of persons we make up and try to hold in some recognizable structure—by which we are at once our talk during waking hours and the dreams we invent, our joking postures and our assumed sincerities, the role-playing we admit to, and the "real" self we are loath to admit is also a form of role-playing —so a writer is at last all the language he uses. The fact that some of it belongs to his fiction makes it no less a part of him, an invention of and by him, than the language he uses in what is crudely designated as nonfiction. All Mailer can mean when he declares that he was "in the act of learning" some truth about America when the same truth abounded years before in his novels is that something happened to him that obliterated the distinction between history and fiction, between writing and action, even while in reporting this development he must illegitimately depend on the distinction.

He is close to a remarkable admission: that he had expected the novelistic form to protect him from retaliations, to protect him in fact from the reality of his own feelings. And indeed his first three novels are each marred by sentimental irresolutions. These are still in evidence at times in *Advertisements for Myself*, as in the passage I have just been considering. The consequence is a prose whose tempo cannot excite the demons and spirits he knows are operating not beneath but within the visible movements of American life. Except sporadically and infrequently, his early prose doesn't bring him in touch with the forces and mysteries he knows he must contend with, and for that reason he can't bring about a satisfactory climax in any of his first three novels.

I quite intend the sexual innuendo. In trying to understand Mailer's troubles in this period and the odd fact that none of these books fulfills itself, it is important to remember that coexistent with his writing and rewriting of *The Deer Park* were the beginnings of what would become his obsession with the orgasm and with some possible equivalence in the masculine effort to create form in writing, in a literary career, and in history. For whatever cause, Mailer came to feel during the mid-1950s, especially while revising *The Deer Park*, that fucking was a metaphor for mounting time, for giving a measure to history—so much so that he could not construe fucking merely as a pleasure. It was an acutely perilous enterprise. Beginning with the revised ending of *The Deer Park*, the idea that there is some relation between sex and time reverberates throughout his work, reaching its theoretical culmination in *The Prisoner of Sex*. One difference between early and later Mailer is that as he chose increasingly to move into the center of his own work he became correspondingly aware that sex might be a metaphor for that act of self-projection which is writing, aware of both writing and fucking as activities by which he could translate the times into his time. The topics sex and time, while being an example of Mailer's repetitiousness, also illustrate, as they pass through the different contexts he was able to provide for them, a decisive change. From being a writer who was content to nurse grievances about his failure to bring it off in America, he becomes a writer who imagines that he can penetrate America's hidden regions and rouse into visible creation the beauties and the monsters that reside there.

Mailer, as usual, knows what he is up to, and the development is acknowledged at least in part by the very title of one of his best stories, written in 1959, "The Time of Her Time." Along with "Advertisements for Myself on the Way Out" of the same year, it was to be part of a long novel, never finished. The novel was, in turn, to be one of eight in a Zolaesque series, wherein Sergius O'Shaugnessy of *The Deer Park* was to be given various roles—there is a psychiatrist named Dr. Sergius in "The Man Who Studied Yoga" which was to serve as a prologue to the eight volumes—and thereby involve himself in the major facets of contemporary American life. Sergius is the self-admiring hero-narrator of "The Time of Her Time." It is his account, as sexual athlete, of his efforts to score with a culturally and psycho-analytically overcommitted coed. By his own testimony he is trying to impart to her the kind of sexual rhythm in which she will find her true liberation; he is trying to make her "come" into history.

In tracing out Mailer's concern for sex and time, a conceptual line can be drawn at least from 1955 and *The Deer Park* through "The Time of Her Time" in 1959 on to *An American Dream* in 1965 and thence to 1971 and *The Prisoner of Sex*. It would of course be convenient to say that what Mailer awaited was a style adequate to the intensely personal complication of these concerns. That is to some extent true, in that he would never again resort to the fatuousness, at once buddy boy and *fin de siècle*, of the end of *The Deer Park*, where, it will be remembered, God is allowed to say in "his weary, cryptic way, 'Rather think of Sex as Time, and Time as the connection of new circuits.'" But the style of a writer never does develop along a line as clearly traceable as the line of his ideas, especially when he is as studious about language as Mailer has been from the beginning of his career. Indeed, many of his arguments about historical or social change are really arguments about changes in the language, changes in verbal fashion: a good third of "The White Negro," for example, is a discussion of the language of Hip.

He is not, then, a writer who shuts off one style and turns on another, and it is too simple to propose that *The Deer Park* marks the culmination of a literary manner which was to give way to the pressures of what needed thereafter to be said. In fact, as I have suggested, it is stylistically retrogressive from some of the tendencies strongly at work in *Barbary Shore*, a rather frightened step back from the prospects opened up now and again by the quite daring writing that goes on, however fitfully, in that book. Politically safe and even smug in its anti-Stalinism, puritanical in its easy collapse of political into sexual degeneracies and perversions, *Barbary Shore* is nonetheless marked by passages of lurid, startling brilliance. For that reason it is especially appealing to those, like myself, who look into the structure of a book hoping to find a clue to the author's sense of analogous social, economic, or political structures. All give a promise of freedom; all prove, at some interesting and locatable point, constricting and repressive.

Where a literary structure proves neither large nor durable enough to give full ventilation to the powers that have been released within it, the likelihood is that the author will not believe that the structures of reality outside his book are any more flexible. Of the characteristics of later Mailer that can be noted in his second novel, none is more pronounced than his desire to write as a kind of liberator, one who creates forms in which there can be a maximum interplay of conflicting and divergent forces. With Hawthorne of the opening of "The New Adam and Eve," Mailer might say, "We who are born into the world's artificial system can never adequately know how little in our present state and circumstances is natural, and how much is merely the interpolation of the perverted mind and heart of man . . . it is only through the medium of the imagination that we can lessen those iron fetters, which we call truth and reality, and make ourselves even partially sensible what prisoners we are."

Barbary Shore, through a melodramatic and rhetorical heightening, makes us aware of possible dimensions of experience of which the rational mind is suspicious, and which totalitarianism is now anxious to erase in the interests of thoroughgoing control through technology and bureaucratization. We are the more aware of the effects of this stylistic daring because the novel is often concerned with matters that Mailer elsewhere treated more quietly or analytically or coolly. In a characterization of the household and of the daily lives of McLeod, Lovett, and Guinevere—a mock Arthurian court—there are, for example, touches of domestic observation, of sensitivity to the dreariness and despair of ordinary impoverished life, that were to reappear, in a sedated version, in "The Man Who Studied Yoga." As another anticipation, the amnesia of Lovett and the necessity that he make a history out of the present means that he is an American hip existentialist almost by default—long before "The White Negro." Similarly, in the debates between McLeod, the Communist agent of prewar vintage, and Hollingsworth, the present agent of American repression, Mailer is skirmishing with his idea that machines are taking over the life of humans and perhaps even have a life of their own—as when McLeod jokes that "if you guard a machine ye're obliged to suffer its anxieties"[3]—an idea to be advanced with zany theoretical seriousness in *Of a Fire on the Moon*. In still other debates between McLeod and Lovett, the "magic at the top" which figures so largely in *An American Dream* is assigned to the bureaucratic managers:

[3] *Barbary Shore*, p. 183.

"Everywhere the bureaucrat has the magic power."[4]
That being the case, and conformity being the result,
Hollingsworth will inherit the world. But, as McLeod
warns him, in terms that have become stock Mailerian,
"You will have merely inherited the crisis, and yours is
the profit of cancer."[5] And along with all this, sex,
politics, and violence as forms of dialectical engagement, each capable of translation into the operations of
the other, are conspicuous throughout the book.

More important than any of these harbingers of the
future, however, are hints of the later style coming now
and then like a promise of what will redeem the mere
repetition of themes and of dialectical oppositions, a
style that begins to mature only in "The White Negro"
and "The Time of Her Time," even though it cannot
quite hold either of them together. The obliteration of
the self in the performance of writing (even though the
pleasure of doing so is somehow made too evident), the
Faulknerian cadences that allow for rapid and yet ma-
jestic changes of focus, the Lawrencian capacity for
evoking ambiance and for imaginative drifts from one
perception to another, the dazzling interpolation of subjects that may have been encouraged by the eccentrici-
ties of Reich and by Mailer's own mixtures of Freud with
Marx but which could not be stylistically indebted to
any of them—these are features of Mailer's style after
The Deer Park which are powerfully to the fore in the
prefatory matter in *Advertisements for Myself*, in "The
White Negro," "The Time of Her Time," and in
"Advertisements for Myself on the Way Out: Prologue
to a Long Novel," with its daring relocations of point of
view, so that the house, objects, persons are variously
suggested as the governing voice. It is not to minimize
the decisive, secured, and accomplished change after
The Deer Park to say that many of these facilities of

4 *Ibid.*, p. 123.
5 *Ibid.*, p. 283.

style, indistinguishable as they are from a growing capacity to think and feel simultaneously at many levels, had been nascent in *Barbary Shore* as in the following, admittedly slight instance. It is an account by Lovett of McLeod's remorse:

> So he continued on and on, expressing at last outwardly the total of all the nights he must have lain in his bed, all nerves alive, limbs aching, while in relentless turmoil each thought birthed its opposite, each object in the darkness swelled with connotation until a chair could contain his childhood, and the warm flaccid body of Guinevere slumbering beside him expanded its bulk to become all women he had ever known, but in their negative aspect, so that whatever pleasure he might have felt was not felt now, and he rooted in all the sweating and lurching of unfulfillment till the flesh of his wife had become just that, and as flesh was the denomination of meat and all the corpses he had ever seen and some created.[6]

Mailer's taste for the long sentence, with all its potentialities for associative rambling, for tributary contributions to the main direction, is evident here and is to become one of the principal resources in *An American Dream*, *The Armies of the Night*, and almost a defect in *Of a Fire on the Moon* and, especially, *The Prisoner of Sex*. For a writer temperamentally committed to discovering improbable links and dialectical interplays, the long sentence is a most attractive instrument, as some later inspections of *Why Are We in Vietnam?* will show. It allows the suspension of a variety of disparate items in a reflective medium wherein, as here, they gradually absorb and enlarge one another. A speculative restraint that comes out in the use of restrictive clauses and negatives, of interjections that break the rhetorical acceleration, of noes and yeses, give such sentences in Mailer the kind of power they lacked in, say, Thomas

[6] *Ibid.*, pp. 239–40.

Wolfe and so conspicuously acquired in Faulkner, who showed Mailer and others how to throttle and release momentum with extraordinary facility. While the examples in *Barbary Shore* are rather elementary, the first fully developed instance perhaps being the third sentence, nearly a page long, in "The Time of Her Time," such sentences are in evidence in this second novel and belong to the larger effort being made in the book to find a stylistic equivalence to the imagined correlation among social, political, and individual psychoses.

Mailer was later to rewrite a passage from Freud, and also one from Marx, showing that, by the substitution of words having to do with social structures for words having to do with psychic ones, it was possible to demonstrate the necessary but neglected similarity between them. The style is appropriately monstrous, but along the way he gives a clue to what he was groping for in *Barbary Shore* and what he has been more successfully trying to do since then: "there is a psychological technique which makes it possible to interpret the unconscious undercurrents of society, and . . . if that procedure is employed, every society reveals itself as a psychical structure which has an unconscious direction or conflict of direction which can be detected at any assignable point in the overt activities of social life."[7] This offers a better excuse for the seemingly insane readings of the world offered by Stephen Rojack in *An American Dream* than it does for the rather more mechanical translations of economic and political theory into sex which are found in *Barbary Shore*. But the very fact that the two books are markedly more similar than is either to *The Deer Park*, gives credence to Mailer's observation that "much of my later writing cannot be understood without a glimpse of the odd shadows and theme-maddened-light *Barbary Shore* casts before it."[8]

[7] *Advertisements for Myself*, p. 438.
[8] *Ibid.*, p. 94.

Some of that "theme-maddened-light" is evident in the passage on McLeod in bed I have quoted above. McLeod's occasional illusion that he might still recover his lost potentialities as a revolutionary are dissipated by recollections of his crimes in the service of the Stalinist terror; similarly his potencies as a lover give way to nightmares of the life he has had to violate for political expediency. In the first instance, the Stalinist revolutionary leftover of the 1930s is hopelessly out of time with the times as represented by the agent of an incipient American totalitarianism, Hollingsworth; sexually he is equally out of time—perhaps, more aptly, out of rhythm ("rooted in all the sweating and lurching of unfulfillment")—so that in the end Hollingsworth is also heir to his wife. Every character in the book is more or less situated in some version of McLeod's agonized failure of synchronization with an ongoing sexual and political time. The only two characters who can make time together, as we have seen, are Hollingsworth and Guinevere, a coupling of sadistic and depraved authoritarianism with materialistic vanity.

Mailer was more despairing in *Barbary Shore* than in *The Naked and the Dead* about the political and sexual futures possible in America. The despair had a tautness which saved him in both cases from mere fashionability, however, and for the reason that he was attracted to the very things a good liberal young man shouldn't like at all: power and obscenity. The one is illustrated in Croft and his assault on Mount Anaka, the other in the sexual looseness and perversity of Guinevere, and, for that matter, of Lannie. Thus poised before *The Deer Park*, Mailer was there relaxed by the inanities and boyish charms of his buddy-hero-narrator, by the too heavily endowed conventions of films and novels about Hollywood, and by the fact that he once again managed to relegate the "worst" elements (which also happened to be the ones that brought forth some of his best energies) to the margin: Marion and Teppis, who is simply more fun than anyone else in the book even while he is supposed to be so symptomatically degenerate.

The play version managed to give Teppis his comic due and also to make something properly powerful out of Marion Faye, even though Eitel is allowed a pompous, priggish, and unscrutinized rejection of Faye's sexual proposition with the speech that "I'd never let a man touch me. I think that's the end of . . . change. It's what all the people who run the machine want us to be. Queer. Queer as cockroaches. Once you want it from behind, there's nothing to do but run. Thanks a lot, Angel, but I don't want to swish."[9] This was written in 1967, sometime after we learn in "The Time of Her Time" that it was nonetheless all right to get the woman up the ass; it might even liberate her from frigidities. Metaphysics about sex tend to dominate Mailer's interest in any kind of sexual intercourse. This is but one instance, of course, of the incipient disproportion in his work between any given human activity and his melodramatic version of it. The disproportion is corrected by moralistic and philosophical rhetoric, and the results are not invariably successful. In the present instance, whether Eitel takes it or leaves it is not a question in which any reader has been made even involuntarily interested; the issue which does matter is that Mailer seems unaware that Eitel's remarks are at best Marcusean sexual-political gibberish.

B. THE TIME OF HIS TIME

Fortunately, "The Time of Her Time" is written in a different key from anything we have been looking at: ebullient, self-pleasuring in its stylistic displays, witty in allusions to Reich and Freud where before there would have been a parsing studiousness, and full of bravado in the face of limitations and failures. All of this can be

[9] *The Deer Park, a Play.*

ascribed to the new identity which Mailer has given his old hero Sergius. And yet one somehow feels even here that Mailer does not release himself from literary, moral, and cultural inheritances as willingly as he does his hero. There is an odd dislocation in the story: its larger claims are made in a rhetoric that has the status of Biblical commentary on an action that is strangely indifferent to it. Put another way, Sergius is indeed Hip but even at this early and enthusiastic point in Mailer's loyalty to the idea, the author is himself not quite that Hip, and he was never to become more so. In Mailer-the-Hip there is always an intellectually nice boy trying to get out and finding, as intellectually nice boys often do, that the safest way to control the merely boisterous, the local and specific pleasure, is by way of metaphysics.

From this point onward—from the late 1950s of "The White Negro" and "The Time of Her Time"—Mailer the Puritan, the Hasidic Jew, the worried copulator, will always be there, moving to the tempo of the hipster and the "swinger." His concern for time and sex always remains within the gravitational pull of the moral references of *Barbary Shore*. Time and sex never belong wholly to the "enormous present." They are claimed equally by a past beyond record and by a future beyond specification. In Mailer the terms "time" and "sex" are not to be thought of chronologically or sequentially but as relatively autonomous states or conditions in space. For that reason, "time" and "sex" are given a status somehow at odds with the story's linear momentum, with the chronological *experience* of sex and of time. Sex as the act of fucking in time has the same problematic relation to sex in space as does Sergius, the hip hero, to Mailer the Creator.

It is not possible to treat the preachments in the story as evidence of a Volponesque outrageousness on Sergius's part. Taken by itself, the story is much more robust, much funnier, much more successfully shaped than when read in the context of Mailer's more philosophical discussions of Hip, sex, and time: notably in "The White Negro" and in *The Prisoner of Sex*. One of the items which outrages Kate Millett and others, for example, is Sergius's reference to his penis as "the avenger." In extenuation it can be said that Mailer has great difficulty in naming the penis in a way agreeable even to male chauvinists—Rojack in *An American Dream* likes to call it his "root," for example—so that perhaps he has a general problem when it comes to the naming of parts. Moreover, Sergius's tone in this instance is meant to be comically exhibitionistic. It is a response to sex with Denise the gladiatorial nature of which is a result more of her conduct than of his. All that allowed, Mailer is still responsible for inventing her, along with her eventually cropped hair, her dungarees with a zipper fly down the front, her flat breasts that swelled, if at all, only to "the convexities of an Amazon's armor." An allusion is intended here to the Reichian idea of body armor, thereby lending some support to Sergius's claim that his "avenger" is an instrument of therapy rather than simple domination.

Whatever way one looks at it, Mailer's inventions are wholly at the service of Sergius. He is the cultural hero as fucker, even when he flatters himself with the homo-erotic idea that the act with Denise is the equivalent of the give and take of two tough club fighters. Boxers, we know, qualify as existential heroes even if they are losers, as Sergius was in the Air Force. But if that were not enough Sergius has also been a bullfighter, whose loft is a bullfighting school in the Village, a lover of exceptional talent, and, by his own designation, "a saint," thanks to his assumed obligation never to send a woman off with a wound in her esteem. Now all of this is no less charming in Sergius than are some corresponding characteristics assigned to Tom Jones, especially since Sergius invents his own mock epic characterization: "the Messiah of the one-night stand."

But it is meant to be more than charming. While

Fielding's language refers us to some classical ideals of another age of which Tom's conduct is a parody, Mailer's refers us to contemporary ideals proposed in his own work and for which Sergius is an authorized representative. Anyone who persists in taking Sergius's language as funny would have to agree to laugh at him because he is hip, and Mailer hardly endorses that; or because he is a ludicrous version of Hip, and that possibility is not allowed either. Two years before, in "The White Negro," Mailer identified the hipster hero in language strikingly identical to the story's characterization of Sergius: "so, too, for the existentialist . . . and the saint and the bull-fighter and the lover. The common denominator for all of them is their burning consciousness of the present, exactly that incandescent consciousness which the possibilities within death have opened for them."[10] Mailer's distinction between the conventional psychopath and the hipster is that the latter "extrapolates from his own condition . . . a radical vision of the universe which thus separates him from the general ignorance, reactionary prejudice, and self-doubt of the more conventional psychopath."[11] Such a requirement might seem rather large for Sergius were it not for the fact that the first section of the story shows him as much more than a mere stick man, of whatever prowess. Before he tries to be a sexual hero he becomes a social one, through carefully contrived confrontations with the perils of a most perilous neighborhood of Blacks and Puerto Ricans—with Jews and Italians nearby, lest anyone accuse Mailer of selective challenges.

It is additionally right, in terms of the prescriptions laid down in "The White Negro," that he should dare the Blacks on their own turf. After all, the hipster has "absorbed the existentialist synapsis of the Negro" and translated it into a kind of fucking that is responsive to more than the tempo of love. It moves to the beat of

[10] *Advertisements for Myself*, p. 342.
[11] *Ibid.*, p. 343.

Negro jazz, where the hip chooses to find "the infinite variations of joy, lust, languor, growl, cramp, pinch, scream and despair of his orgasm."[12] Still more, Sergius's report that while holding a nineteen-year-old girl's ass he is "hefting those young kneadables of future power" is verbally if not physiologically appropriate to the suggestion in the essay that "the hipster has shifted the focus of his desire from immediate gratification toward that wider passion for future power that is the mark of the civilized man."[13] As it turns out, Sergius is not merely trying to have an orgasm with Denise; he does that frequently enough with her without feeling like a failure. Instead, he wants to be the first to make her have a complete orgasm, to make her at last enter "the time of her Time." Only if he succeeds in doing this will he win a kind of *future* power accrued to him from the experience. Precisely for that reason he feels like a white Negro competing with some supposititious "bearded Negro cat who would score where I had missed and thus cuckold me in spirit, deprive me of those telepathic waves of longing (in which I obviously believe) speeding away to me from her over the years to balm the hours when I was beat, because I had been her psychic bridegroom, had plucked her ideational diddle, had led her down the walk of her real wedding night."[14]

Sergius, that is, is looking for love, much as is Rojack in *An American Dream* who also believes in "telepathic waves." They allow him to communicate at the very end of the book with the dead Cherry. The requirements for love only superficially involve finding a mate who pleases. There must also be, again in the words of "The White Negro," "the search for an orgasm more apocalyptic than the one which preceded it."[15] As so

[12] *Ibid.*, p. 341.
[13] *Ibid.*, p. 343.
[14] *Ibid.*, p. 496.
[15] *Ibid.*, p. 347.

often, Mailer's language somehow belies, on a closer look, any simple inference drawn from its exhortatory tones. Note that the orgasm is something not accomplished so much as "searched for." It is really never wholly successful. There is mystery within sex, as readers of Emily Brontë already know, which helps account for its power to make "psychic bridegrooms" more important after many years than the eventual real ones. And the mystery is that sex proposes "the paradise of limitless energy and perception just beyond the next wave of the next orgasm."[16] Quite a ways off even for a white Negro and even further for any nice couple who think they're enjoying one another: "beyond the next wave of the next . . ." Indeed, it's as much Romeo and Juliet, dying happily ever after, as Heathcliff and Cathy.

The imagination of Hip is a distinctly adolescent one, though that is in no sense to its discredit. So, too, is the language of hip. While hipsters are said by Mailer to be a very small elite—of ten million American psychopaths (so he guessed in 1957) no more than 100,000 are conscious hipsters. It is these who speak "a language most adolescents can understand instinctively."[17] Hipsters are like children in giving expression to the buried infant in themselves. They are redeemed from mere infantilism or from a petrified adolescence, however, because they truly seek some version of what William James meant by a second birth or, in Mailer's phrase, the chance "to grow up a second time."[18] The language of Hip "is a language of energy,"[19] he tells us, thus offering a rationale for the tone of Sergius. More than that, it explains Mailer's own new intensifications and elaborations of style when he deals with ideas that were themselves not new for him. One can therefore understand his distaste for the spurious language of youth, adoles-

16 *Ibid.*, p. 351.
17 *Ibid.*, p. 343.
18 *Ibid.*, p. 346.
19 *Ibid.*, p. 349.

cence, or childhood that was to evolve in the 1960s and that he was to hear in the Washington of *The Armies of the Night* and the Chicago of *Miami and the Siege of Chicago*, a language full of sloganeering cant, of uninventive obscenities, of onanistic disengagements in such phrases as "doing your own thing," or "oh, gee, wow" with its pile-up of puerile ejaculations. When he listened to the language really spoken by the young—so very few of whom could ever qualify to be called Hip—Mailer became aware, as he has so often been made aware, of how seldom reality measures up to his imagination of it. Not merely the orgasm but a good deal of everything he imagines must exist, I'm afraid, "beyond the next wave of the next . . ."

The discontinuities between Sergius's tone and the role given him as theologian indicate how Mailer's pet ideas are allowed a quite precarious, sometimes nearly discredited position within his style. It is extraordinarily difficult to determine where, in a given instance, he wants his weight to be felt or where he is making some major investment. Far from being emphatic at all times, he is quite often engagingly elusive. He is full of disclaimers in all his later work, starting with "The White Negro." "Because, after all, what I have offered above is an hypothesis, no more, and there is not the hipster alive who is not absorbed in his own tumultuous hypotheses."[20] "Because, after all" is not the tone of apocalyptic, revolutionary, or dogmatic proselytizing, and the word "tumultuous" suggests that even his hypotheses have a hypothetical existence. At another point in the essay he proposes that in reducing life to its ultimate alternatives, the present century may be preparing for the last war of all between "the blacks and the whites, or between the women and the men, or between the beautiful and ugly, the pillagers and managers, or the rebels and the regulated." His inclusion in this not otherwise wholly

[20] *Ibid.*, p. 351.

implausible list of "the beautiful and ugly" is itself a near total cop-out. But even then he chooses to add a more general and indicative bit of shyness and slyness: "which of course is carrying speculation beyond the point where speculation is still serious, and yet despair at the monotony and bleakness of the future have become so engrained in the radical temper that the radical is in danger of abdicating from all imagination."[21]

This sentence proposes a wholly spurious alternative. Mailer is saying, as he will more and more often, and with something close to shrillness by *Of a Fire on the Moon*, that his imagination (for there is no other radical speaking here) is the only alternative to other, historically operative and, by inference, repressive and disfiguring powers. His campaign for Mayor of New York was serious to the degree that in it he was saying the same thing. Essentially he did not mean that New York City should elect him its Mayor so that he could live in Gracie Mansion and negotiate the garbage pick-ups. Rather he meant: elect me as the Imagination of your future in the otherwise sure prospect of "monotony and bleakness." Our hypothetical vote depends, therefore, on whether or not his writing can make us assent to magnifications of elements in ourselves and in contemporary life that it may be in our own interest to miniaturize. Our motive for this miniaturization may be fear but it may also be a conviction that the proportions of life promise more as they are now than they would if we reconceived them in the shape offered by Mailer's imagination.

This is a critical question that is central to Mailer's whole provocative and crafty enterprise. "The White Negro" is, most simply, a magnification of the repressed minority of Blacks and, more specifically, Black psychopaths, into what "could become the central expression of human nature before the twentieth century is over."[22]

21 *Ibid.*, p. 357.
22 *Ibid.*, p. 345.

Even at this level of celestial gaseousness, the concept of hip is more daring than Jean Malaquais made it out to be when he complained that the hipster was simply a substitute for the proletariat of an earlier radical critique. It is also more threatening (or promising) than a mere prediction of some eventual shift in social and cultural hierarchies. What Mailer is appealing to is a time-honored pastoral yearning for some earlier state, even while suggesting that what we miss is not our lost simplicity. The technetronic age will be glad to restore that. What we miss is our lost complexity and inner conflict. The "Negro" is the child in all of us, but the child after Freud, and the essay is a call to us to become "children" not that we might escape from time but that we might re-engage ourselves with it. We must face again the "hopeless contradictions [we] knew as an infant and as a child."[23] I suspect that these "hopeless contradictions" refer in part to a painful fact about human beings: that from birth they are both more retarded in bodily development and, in relation to that development, more sexually precocious than any other animal. A human being meets this progressive crisis of discontinuity—of wanting what Reich calls end-pleasure before being physically capable of achieving it—through the development of sexual repression.

Sexual repression can thus be explained in a way congenial to Mailer the metaphysician: as a biological rather than historical mechanism, or as an organic necessity however much it might be aggravated by institutional forces. In this respect he would tend even this early to be radically conservative, more like Geza Roheim, a psychoanalytic anthropologist he very probably hasn't read, than like Marcuse, who would trace the damage done the libido to correctable economic and political forces of repression. Mailer is deeply suspicious of psychoanalysis because it treats as ills conflicts that

[23] *Ibid.*, p. 346.

he regards as part of nature and thus irremediable (that the heroine of "The Time of Her Time" is deep in analysis is not in her favor). It is a tranquilizer of frictions within the self and within society which ought rather to be exacerbated. He would magnify what civilization tends to disguise, and this includes the reasons to fear death, the dread of the unknown. Fear and dread belong to the collective psyche of the race upon which a rationalistic technology is mounting its final offensive.

"Collective" is a word used very frequently by Mailer; it effectively describes the dimensions for him of even the smallest individual act; it proposes, even more, our immense responsibility for the way we choose to dispose of our individual lives or submit to the disposal of them by others. In this as in so many other respects his works echo the old American Puritans. Their presence is especially felt in a passage from "The White Negro" (cited with special admiration in one of the early and still one of the best essays on Mailer, by Diana Trilling):

> The Second World War presented a mirror to the human condition which blinded anyone who looked into it. For if tens of millions were killed in concentration camps out of the inexorable agonies and contradictions of superstates founded upon the always insoluble contradictions of injustice, one was then obliged also to see that no matter how crippled and perverted an image of man was the society he had created, it was nonetheless his creation, his collective creation (at least his collective creation from the past) and if society was so murderous, then who could ignore the most hideous of questions about his own nature?[24]

Attention expands outward from "one's own nature" past superstates to the collective nature of man and reverberates back again, confirming an observation by

[24] *Ibid.*, p. 338.

James Toback that God and the Devil, Good and Evil, Heaven and Hell, History and Eternity are as inescapably real for Mailer as they were for Jonathan Edwards. Potentially seeing everything within terms of such magnitude, he can unabashedly through Sergius, and with a wit not meant to be at all satiric, call a woman's ass "those young kneadables of future power," or treat social manners in *An American Dream* as if they belonged to a celestial struggle between God and the Devil.

Characters like Sergius, Rojack, D. J. and Tex in *Why Are We in Vietnam?*—along with Mailer as a character in his work—are all placed close enough to the familiar, to what is considered ordinary, so that their deviations from it will be a challenge and an aggravation. They are "real" enough while simultaneously being lower-depths versions of the central man, so that we have to wonder whether or not the central man now truly exists only in the lower depths. Like characters in *The Naked and the Dead* and *The Deer Park*, these later ones are endowed with features that belong to the world in which the reader can claim a place, even a dominion, while they are also citizens of another, mysterious, and, to some readers, quite puerile world of childish daydreams —as if childish daydreams were not an essential part of all of us, of our national and cultural myths.

Near to the surface, these myths or daydreams or fantasies of power are ready to assert themselves whenever the exercise of nature and civilized power proves useless in coping with the organized, even placid insanity of contemporary institutions. The ingredients in Mailer's work will seem perhaps too familiar, even too pop or "trendy," only to those who don't get the point. No special sentiment, no shared opinion is required; nothing more than the attention legitimately called for by the most accomplished ventriloquist of styles now writing in English. It is difficult to read him with any sympathy unless one reads with great closeness, looking for that ability he credits to James Jones: "The nicest thing about Jim as a writer is his ease in moving from mystical to practical reaction with his characters. Few novelists can do this, it's the hint of greatness."[25]

Indeed it is, and it is what Mailer attempts at some point in every book he has written, most successfully in *An American Dream*, *The Armies of the Night*, and *Why Are We in Vietnam?* It is central, this effort, to his claims for heroism as an artist and to the dialectical nature of his style. Speaking, again, of the language of hip, he revealingly remarks that "it is a pictorial language, but pictorial like non-objective art, imbued with the dialectic of small but intense change, a language for the microcosm, in this case, man, for it takes the immediate experience of any passing man and magnifies the dynamic of his movements, not specifically but abstractly so that he is seen more as a vector in a network of forces than as a static character in a crystallized field. (Which latter is the practical view of the snob.)"[26]

This is meant as an aid to the uninitiated in their encounter with Hip language, especially with words that define human states according to degrees and kinds of motion, like "creep" or "turn on," or "go," or "put down" or "groove on." Mobility is the clue, in fact, to his interjected crack about the snob. For Mailer an essential element in Hip, and in the styles of Hip, is that it involves nearly unimpeded movement across social barriers. Not only minority persons, but minority or repressed feelings can, when set in motion, at least temporarily disrupt inherited or economically grounded positions of status. Mailer's conception of hip style helps explain his own as it developed out of *Barbary Shore* and through the inertias of *The Deer Park*, and into the kind of writing he has done since. He was to tell Richard Stern in 1958, about a year after "The White Negro," that "what attracts me about Hip is that it's involved with more expression, with getting into the

[25] *Cannibals and Christians*, p. 113.
[26] *Advertisements for Myself*, pp. 348–49.

nuances of things." And when Stern asks, "More expression or more experience?" he replies:

> The two have an umbilical relationship. What makes a novelist great is that he illumines each line of his work with the greatest intensity of experience. One thing about Hip you have to admit is that the hipster lives in a state of extreme awareness, and so objects and relations that most people take for granted become terribly charged for him; and, living in a state of self-awareness, his time slows up. His page becomes more filled. The quality of his experience becomes more intense. That doesn't make for less expression; it makes for greater difficulty of expression. It makes for writing more pages about fewer episodes which is certainly not the quintessence of the inarticulate.[27]

For Mailer in his writing, as much as for the Hip in his language, experience and expression are synchronized. In fact, no experience in and of itself qualifies as Hip until or unless language makes it so. Language can thus quite randomly take "the experiences of any passing man" and by a fairly systematized vocabulary set about to "magnify the dynamic of his movement, not specifically but abstractedly . . ." Just as the language of a hipster *is* the experience which is Hip, so the writing of Mailer *is* the experience of a Rojack or a Sergius or a D. J. or a Mailer. It is known for what it is in the language which invents it, and not otherwise known. The language is, then, not a reference to experience. To read Mailer as if the language were a series of referential signs is wholly to misread him, to make him an obnoxious puffer.

Each character or item in Mailer's work since the mid-1950s is magnified by his effort to illumine the page, to make the page "filled," and his quite proper justification for this is that each thing really is much more than it seems to be or is taken to be. It is a "vector in a net-

[27] *Ibid.*, p. 379.

work of forces." The network is of course only his language, his creation, but it is insistently evocative of forces that have to be imagined as at least possibly at work in the political, sexual, psychic life of the times. The grandmother with orange hair in *The Armies of the Night*, the hippies or Mayor Daley in *Miami and the Siege of Chicago*, the various political and athletic figures in *The Presidential Papers* and *Cannibals and Christians* are all described with great deftness of allusion because for Mailer they bring into focus elements from various sectors of American life which are called out of hiding, as it were, at times of political or other public extravaganzas. Thus of Scranton in his try for President: "One felt he had been spoiled when he was young by a lack of testing. It was not that he lacked bravery, it was that he had lacked all opportunity to be brave for much too long, and now he was not so much engaged in a serious political struggle as in a puberty rite."[28] Or the prediction that Philip Roth will be called the "rich man's Paddy Chayefsky, and Paddy without his grasp of poverty is nothing much at all."[29] Or his historical zooming away from and then close up to the gangster chiefs hanging around Sonny Liston's training camp: "There were also some fine old mafiosos whose faces one had seen on busts of Venetian doges in the Ducal Palace, subtle faces, insidious with the ingrowth of a curious culture built on treachery, dogma, the evil eye, and blood loyalty to the clan."[30] Or the remarkable characterization of Lyndon Johnson in 1960, well before he became a national scandal: "There was Johnson who had compromised too many contradictions and now the contradictions were in his face: when he smiled the corners of his mouth squeezed gloom; when he was pious, his eyes twinkled irony; when he spoke in a righteous tone, he looked corrupt; when he jested, the ham in

[28] *Cannibals and Christians*, p. 15.
[29] *Ibid.*, p. 122.
[30] *The Presidential Papers*, p. 224.

his jowls looked to quiver."[31] These are rather simple examples of Mailer's capacity to assemble at a given point all the contributory cultural lore that makes a single figure or event into a more generally significant one. His is an imagination which even while it rejects the conglomerating power of technology and the media is also trying to surpass it.

In the prefatory matter written for *Advertisements for Myself*, in *The Presidential Papers*, and in most of the pieces that were collected in *Cannibals and Christians*, all of which preceded the best so far—*An American Dream*, *Why Are We in Vietnam?*, and *The Armies of the Night*—Mailer's imagination began to be exercised in direct and imitative competition with the powers that he sees as most damaging to the imagination and to life. His genius became manifest in the exploratory linkages of images and ideas that were to evolve in still later works into too systematic an account of the mysteries of existence. The very movement of his language from about 1959 onward was intended to counter "that civilization founded upon the Faustian urge to dominate nature by mastering time, mastering the links of social cause and effect."[32]

Precisely such mastery is what Mailer strives for in his writing—or in sex, more specifically in creative orgasm. The difference between the mastery sought for in Mailer's prose and the Faustian urge of contemporary civilization is that he wishes to put himself and us in touch with the contradictions, mysteries, and dreads that civilization based on technology is trying to disguise. But the effort demands that he set up a terminology and a system of references very often alien to rationalistic thinking. To make the usual kind of sense is for Mailer only to subscribe to the Faustian mastery of the links of cause and effect. It is to conform to the time sequences and rhythms that lead

[31] *Ibid.*, p. 35.
[32] *Advertisements for Myself*, p. 338.

to cancer and totalitarianism. The first is a proliferation of sameness, which is death to the imagination; the second is insistence on uniformity, which relaxes the dialectical tensions that are, he thinks, essential to life.

Since I will be demonstrating in the next chapter the kind of positive achievement which results from Mailer's efforts to seize control of the links of social cause and effect, I want to indicate here some of the unfortunate consequences. They are most evident in his discussions of sex. His rather heavy and fearsome attitudes on the subject result, I think, from a curious connection in his mind between sexual careers and the career of the novelist, between sexual creativity and the creative effort to shape history. For Mailer, a love affair is the elemental and most demanding of all dialectical relationships, and even a one-night stand can be enormously important so long as something is at stake—one's fear of inadequacy, the desire or dread of conceiving another child, or that complex of feelings provoked in *The Armies of the Night* by his meeting Paul Goodman:

> Goodman's ideas tended to declare in rough that heterosexuality, homosexuality, and onanism were equally valid forms of activity, best denuded of guilt. Mailer, with his neo-Victorianism, thought that if there was anything worse than homosexuality and masturbation, it was putting the two together. The super-hygiene of all this mental prophylaxis offended him profoundly. Super-hygiene impregnated the air with medicated Vaseline—there was nothing dirty in the damn stuff; and sex to Mailer's idea of it was better off dirty, damned, even slavish! than clean, and without guilt. For guilt was the existential edge of sex. Without guilt, sex was meaningless. One advanced into sex against one's sense of guilt, and each time guilt was successfully defied, one had learned a little more about the contractual relation of one's own existence to the unheard thunders of the deep—each time guilt herded one back with its authority, some primitive awe—hence some creative clue to the rages of the

deep—was left to brood about. Onanism and homosexuality were not, to Mailer, light vices—to him it
sometimes seemed that much of life and most of
society were designed precisely to drive men deep into
onanism and homosexuality; one defied such a fate
by sweeping up the psychic profit which derived from
the existential assertion of yourself—which was a way
of saying that nobody was born a man; you earned
manhood provided you were good enough, bold
enough.[33]

This is already the prisoner of sex, but in Marlboro
Country: "provided you were good enough, bold
enough." I would suppose that anyone not overawed by
such rhetorical summonings as "the thunders of the
deep" (which next time round must, of course, become
"the rages of the deep") will find this passage unsatis-
factory. Any discussion of "sex" probably ought to
involve some discriminations as to its various forms.
When any attempt is made, as by Kinsey or by Masters
and Johnson, it excites the contempt of those who think
that to make an effort at even preliminary measurements,
in an area where we are fantastically ignorant, is somehow to do an injustice to a mystery—as if it were somehow a degradation of the heavens to study the stars.
Such mystery is best maintained, I am afraid, where
verbal precision is least respected, and in this passage
there is some of the frequent blurring that goes on in
The Prisoner of Sex and elsewhere, until "sex,"
"orgasm," "creation," "love," "fucking" are made to
service one another in an orgy of language. To what
aspects of "sex" in this passage does he mean "guilt" to
apply? Is it to heterosexual fornication as well as to
onanism? If more to the latter, then how much more
and why? Does it apply to buggery with women as well
as with men? If not, why not? To fellatio as much as to
buggery? Does it matter, sexual identities aside, who

[33] *The Armies of the Night*, pp. 24–25.

has done what to whom when it comes to feeling properly guilty?

These are important questions to someone raised, say, in the Catholic Church and for whom Mailer might very often sound like a priest of the Inquisition—and a convert, at that—but they should occupy anyone who wonders what a style so compelling as Mailer's is trying to do. For if these specific questions are thought idle, then what is left is the simple proposition that for Mailer, the neo-Victorian, all forms of sexual activity are tinged with guilt. But this is far too simple; his very commitments to the style in which he characteristically writes would not permit him to be so flat-minded. Let us grant, then, that for some people—and it would be interesting to know for how many—during certain sexual activities there is a feeling of what can be called "primitive awe" about one's place in the creation, awe compounded by the consciousness that humans are perhaps the only animals who can feel anything more than physical gratification in the sexual act. Nonetheless, the word "guilt," far from being the best or even a good word to describe that feeling, is a really heinous one.

Clearly, it is not a very useful word here, and it is worth wondering why it seemed to Mailer necessary and convenient. I suspect that he is not really anxious, at this particular point, to talk about guilt as it might apply to sex. What he is probably saying is that anyone under the tutelage of Paul Goodman should feel guilty because Goodman does not feel awe in the practice or contemplation of sexual intercourse. Actually it is Goodman who should feel guilty. And why? Because he does not feel about sex the way Mailer feels.

Let me insist that I am not arguing about Mailer's motives or suggesting some hidden cause for his argument; I am rather trying to explore the workings and the consequences of his style in this passage. What happens here is a fair enough example of how he gets himself involved in a subject. It also shows that his mind is possessed of an unrelieved anxiety: his fear that he might be confused with someone else, that he might not decisively enough even exist, that his revolutionary stance will not appear wholly original. It is to be remembered that Mailer is reporting his reaction to Goodman during a party at the home of some Washington liberals, and that they are both scheduled to speak later on the same program and to march together in the same protest of October 1967 against the war in Vietnam. Both are attending and, as the title of the chapter wittily suggests, both are members of "The Liberal Party." Except that Mailer is whatever he means by a left conservative. Just before the discussion of sex and guilt, he had found another reason to criticize Goodman even while praising his militancy: "But, oh, the style! It set Mailer's teeth on edge to read it; he was inclined to think that the body of students who followed Goodman must have something de-animalized to put up with the style or at least such was Mailer's bigoted view." What he means by "the style" is clarified somewhat later, in the chapter called "In the Rhetoric," where, as in the later *Miami and the Siege of Chicago*, he is concerned with the language of the American protest movement and of the young. As in his discussion of sex, his critique of language is ultimately a defense of neglected mysteries and visions of which liberal rationality takes no sufficient notice. The language he finds most offensive smells

like the storeroom of a pharmacology company's warehouse, doubtless productive of cancer over the long haul, but essential perhaps, perhaps! to a Left forever suffering from malnutrition. Mailer knew this attitude had nothing to do with reality—if names like SANE or Women Strike for Peace sounded like brand names which could have been used as happily to sell aspirin, he could hardly think the same of SNCC or SDS or one or two of the others; now and again, remarkable young men sprang out of these alphabet soups. No, it was more that the Novelist begrudged the dimming of what was remarkable in the best of these young men because some part of their nervous system would have to attach vision and lust and dreams of power, glory, justice, sacrifice, and future purchases on heaven to these deadening letters.[34]

It's the Novelist he's worried about. Behind the ostensible subjects of sex, language, and style is the central concern about where Mailer the Novelist fits into the revolutionary alliance. More aptly, he is searching for the ways in which Mailer the Novelist does *not* fit into any easy alliance. How could he be expected to fit, having designated himself as the Novelist responsible for values no other kind of writer, except possibly a poet, necessarily has to care about—the Imagination, dread, awe, wonder, mystery? Throughout *Of a Fire on the Moon* he conditions himself to feel differently from the journalists with whom he is regularly assigned to work. The effort can be rather pathetic, as during the Von Braun press speech, where he tries to imagine some special relationship to the speaker, and likely comic, as in his postfight meeting with Liston in "The Eleventh Presidential Paper—Death," where Mailer actually shoulders himself past the press corps, to a ludicrous confrontation of whispered insults and promises with the new champion.

This impulse toward assertion, this fear of extinction, is important in explaining how such incidents occur and how such passages get written. But of much greater importance is the fact that the drive to give Mailer the Novelist a unique position within an occasion can be said actually to structure his thinking when he gets round to reproducing the occasion in writing. Thus the status of his ideas depends all too often on his will to differentiate the lone Novelist from the mass of fellow journalists, and especially the lone left-conservative-

[34] *Ibid.*, p. 95.

revolutionary from liberals posing as revolutionaries. Thinking, in Mailer's writings, is a function of other things that are normally thought to follow from it. It is the function of his desperate need to imagine himself the savior of the imagination and, inevitably in whatever circumstance, a minority figure.

The passages under consideration occur in a book where Mailer very willingly joins a protest march, joins with other dissenters or revolutionaries, and all through it, even in jail, pictures himself as at odds with his compatriots. Much more instinctively, he feels compatible with those who are supposed to be his opponents: the cops, especially when they are U. S. marshals, the judge he is so anxious to impress when he is called before the bench, the badgered and exploited soldiers who guard the Pentagon against which the whole march of collegiates, intellectuals, and the privileged is directed. He is in the eloquently patriotic situation of a man who feels the competing pulls of America in him, the worst in the best, the best in the worst of it. His situation is less important, of itself, again, than the language that emanates from it. In the passages about Goodman and about the slogans of the protest organizations his elementary response seems to be essentially scatological. In the "liberal party" and in the dissenting organizations he finds thinking (what he calls their love of concepts) separated from obscenity, sex separated from dreams of some ultimate "scream and pinch of orgasm," vision separated from lust, justice from love of power. In a quite laudable way he sets out in his writing to restore these missing or neglected or spurned qualities to what he considers their rightful and seductive place in the scheme of things.

Their seductive, their necessary place is in a dialectical opposition to the prevailing mood, particularly if it is a nice and vegetarian mood, a reminder, perhaps, of those same qualities in himself that he has been at such pains to get rid of. That nice boy whom Mailer remembers with some embarrassment was salvaged, after all, by having been in an army quite unlike the one in which the Harvard graduate and distinguished author now finds himself obliged to march. It was not an army of liberals and of "drug-vitiated jargon-mired children"[35] but of mostly Southern boys, average pals and buddies, "real" American teen-agers. They were fellows to be loved and admired with a proper wit. If the present "army" is of a quite different sort, if it is dominated by "concepts," the earlier one was redolent of "obscenity," and Mailer, as he marches with one army against a later version of the other, still admits that he "never felt more like an American than when he was naturally obscene— all the gifts of the American language came out in the happy play of obscenity against concept, which enabled one to go back to concept again."[36]

"Happy play" of this kind is often the effect of Mailer's own style, personal as well as literary. It helps account for the already noted agitation within him between the modest or nice or clean boy, on the one hand, and, on the other, the man who courts the funky and the odoriferous, who wants to get back from the "liberal party" in Washington to a quite different party in New York that has "every promise of being wicked, tasty, and rich."[37] In addition, it characterizes that best kind of interplay which will hold the country together. In effect Mailer makes himself into the country—the Brooklyn Jew, Harvard graduate, Army rifleman, novelist, dialectician, brawler, father, and at the time, in 1968, married to a woman who makes him think "that no, it could not be an altogether awful country because otherwise how would his wife, a Southerner and an Army brat, have come out so subtle, so supple, so mysterious, so fine-skinned, so tender and wise."[38]

[35] *Ibid.*, p. 280.
[36] *Ibid.*, p. 48.
[37] *Ibid.*, p. 84.
[38] *Ibid.*, p. 171.

It is not too much to say that Mailer regards his style as an image of America as well as of himself: ideally it includes both "concept" and "obscenity," Northern Wasp and Southern GI, and the mix varies with the context which occasions it. *The Armies of the Night* is mostly about Mailer's *in*capacity on the spot to achieve the kind of proper mix apparently possible only in the writing done after the event. During the time in Washington, D. C., he was continually interrupted, put down, forced into politeness, silent and sullen by turns, made to listen to noises he is not making, or to make noises he finds immediately unnatural. As an example, there is the Ambassador Theater meeting where he finds he has been displaced as MC, proves an embarrassment when he takes over, and hears himself in his speech use the phrase "bless us all." When he picks up most of his applause on the word "bless," he repeats the phrase with the characteristic addition: "bless us all—shit!" The audience, he has told us a page earlier, "were middle-class cancer-pushers and drug-gutted flower children," who had "Paul Goodman to lead them."[39] Here, as so often, Mailer nominates himself as the "obscene" minority in opposition to an alliance which, as it often turns out, he has previously joined, has helped to make, or even leads. (A rather startling instance occurred at the kickoff for Mailer's mayoralty campaign early in the summer of 1969. Having circulated amiably throughout the group, he then took the platform and within ten minutes, sensing that the audience of socialite supporters and prep-schooled Ivy-leagued hippies were taking him too much for granted, were assuming a too easy alliance between him and them, he first abused them for their anticipated laziness and then, his body pushed out in a boyish schoolyard pugnacity, stood there shouting "Fuck you" to a chorus back of the same.)

What is one to conclude from this? Only in writing

[39] *Ibid.*, p. 35.

can Mailer exist in a form that embraces his contradictions; only in writing about a historical occasion after it is over can he give form to feelings that, expressed at the time, threaten to mutilate the form he is searching for in the occasion. The time of his time probably has no historical equivalent, only a literary one. The form of history most tolerable to him is made of his own language existing in a kind of suspension, productive of a turmoil of meaning that public events are designed not to sustain but to ameliorate.

Men of great power and magnificent ambition, men who become Presidents or champions of the world, are, if one could look into their heads, men very much like Mailer. But they make a point of not letting us, as he does, look into their heads. Their madness may be their motive, but it is not their image to the world. Mailer is fascinated by dialectical encounters in which hunger for power, fascination with mystery, and any kind of lust all work to the possible destruction of opponents rather than the destruction of oneself. Dialectics are his hope of sanity. Existing uncomfortably as a mere person rather than what he calls a Being, a mere character—partial, moderated—his only alternative outside writing is to turn destructively round on himself with scatology. Where Mailer is not, by virtue of the act of writing, able to control a situation, the hidden thrust of his energy is toward the sacrificial waste of himself, toward shit.

As words go, "shit" is a very good one. It is one of the best now available in opposition to the hygienic-cosmetic denaturing of life carried out at the behest of modern technologies; and it is obviously an eloquent word of protest in that it accurately enough describes the end result of the practices it condemns. And yet writing would not exist if any word, even the Word, were enough. The word "god" like the word "shit" is no more than the cry of inarticulateness in search of a theology.

A theology of sorts is what Mailer, since at least "The White Negro," has been constructing, and like other theologies his proposes an order of time markedly different from the one he can treat scatologically. Literary occurrences of a similar scatological-theological pattern lead back to Dante and the asshole of Satan, to Spenser and the Cave of Mammon, to the Luther of Erik Erikson, to Swift and the "Filthy Lucre" of Norman O. Brown, to Coleridge, Thoreau, Burroughs, and Beckett. Mailer's theological schemes are both more extemporized and, to correct resultant instabilities, finally more confiningly systematic than any of these others. His is involved in an attempt to correlate the activities of sex and writing, and to see in both the opportunity, otherwise denied by the forces of corporate power, to give some individual shaping, always within the confines of language, to history and to the passage of time.

This brings us to the most recent and most blatant efforts in this direction: *The Prisoner of Sex* and *Of a Fire on the Moon*. Aside from the fact that both books were published in 1970–1971, they belong together on more substantial grounds. Both are about the deformations of the body and the atrophy of the senses which result, as Mailer sees it, from the technologizing of human existence. Of course, opinions of this kind can be found as far back as the oppositions to finance capitalism in the age of Elizabeth, and its evolution into theories of sexual repression is elaborated from Freud's *Civilization and Its Discontents* by Reich and by Marcuse. But the possible sources for Mailer's thinking are less important than is its derivation from his own prior sense of role as a Novelist, from his conviction that writing is a kind of combative enterprise analogous to war. He is involved in an imagined war between God and the Devil, Nature and Technology, Creativity and Waste for control of the links of cause and effect, and he positioned himself for this as early as *The Naked and the Dead.* "Actually man is in transit between brute and God"[40] according to General Cummings, and "had to destroy God in order to achieve Him, equal Him."[41]

Both Croft, with his "odd dreams and portents of power," his "vistas of omnipotence,"[42] and Cummings, who tells Lieutenant Hearn, "You know, if there is a God, he's just like me,"[43] are important prefigurations of the power Mailer wishes to combat. They also prefigure the kind of power that will enthrall him, though they are rather too primitively individualistic to represent it in a compelling way. Indeed, they fail because their efforts are curiously isolated, uncoordinated to a machine. General Cummings may be correct when he writes that perhaps certain kinds of machines have personalities and that "we are not so discrete from the machine any longer,"[44] but the hypothesis could not be effectively demonstrated in World War II or soon thereafter as a unique consequence of historical accelerations that were in fact only to occur later. His demonstrations of humans as part of a machine in this first novel are therefore not much more contemporary than are Stephen Crane's in *The Red Badge of Courage.* No wonder, then, that Cummings' words are resurrected with such relief, and with so little embarrassment at their repetition, twenty-five years later, to account for the enterprise of the moonshot in *Of a Fire on the Moon.* By that point, Cummings' vision has been substantiated by the computers, both in what they are and in what they measure. The Faustian enterprise which had before been merely quixotic has, in the technetronic age, become corporate and therefore rational. This development, too, was anticipated in *The Naked and the Dead.* In reaction to a smug letter from a Washington-

[40] *The Naked and the Dead*, p. 323.
[41] *Ibid.*, p. 392.
[42] *Ibid.*, p. 40.
[43] *Ibid.*, p. 183.
[44] *Ibid.*, p. 569.

based college friend, claiming that the political Right is everywhere in retreat, Lieutenant Hearn proposes, as if for Mailer, that

> . . . there were powerful men in America, on the march and aroused, some of them perhaps even conscious in their particular dream. And the tools were all ready to hand, the men like his father, the ones who would function in instinctive accord, not knowing, not even caring where the road led them. It could be narrowed probably to a dozen, two dozen men, not even in communication with each other, not even all on the same level of awareness.
>
> But it was much more than that. You could kill the dozen men, and there would be another dozen to replace them, and another and another. Out of all the vast pressures and cross currents of history was evolving the archetype of twentieth-century man.[45]

Almost in illustration, the campaign on the island is brought to a successful conclusion in the absence of the man who planned it: Cummings is visiting Army Headquarters on another island, and the operation is supervised by the mere bumbling functionary Major Dalleson. The whole war is mostly run by the "American college intellectuals" who "were all in the government now," Hearn thinks; they will later appear at a space-control headquarters outside Houston, still answering to Hearn's description of twenty-five years before, with their "incisive but always peripheral information, and the dry dejuiced hopelessness of all of them with their rational desiccated minds and their wistful contemplation of lusts and evils they would never understand with their bodies. William Blake angels, gray and clear, hovering over horseshit."[46] Desexualization and integration are, in Mailer, the psychic and political prerequisites of technology from the very outset, and the "single permissive sexual standard," of which he accuses advo-

[45] *Ibid.*, p. 391.
[46] *Ibid.*, p. 240.

cates of Women's Liberation in *The Prisoner of Sex*, is itself a metaphor for integration, for the dissolution of differences and, finally, of the dialectics so precious to him.

Locating in opponents the similarities that secretly attract them to one another and in allies the differences that guarantee the salt of their relationship, is one of Mailer's tactics for achieving some measure of always active coherence in his writing—and it is a tactic, too, for proposing a possible political life for the Republic. A single permissive standard in anything is, for him, not only deadening but pernicious, the expression of what Marcuse calls repressive desublimination and what Mailer himself identifies as left totalitarianism, a label he affixes to Kate Millett. For Mailer the technology revolution has managed to blur most of the political lines which emerge from the last great, and failed, political revolution in 1917. The conspiracy to regiment and pacify life has subsequently united the technologically driven systems of East and West regardless of their political differences, which are fast disappearing anyway.

This redrawing of political boundaries, which helps explain Mailer's impatience with the liberal pro-American, anti-Communist dichotomy of the 1950s, and his recognition of the betrayal in this period of the possibilities of a political and sexual revolution, appeared early in his work. It can be found in "David Reisman Reconsidered" of 1954, in "The White Negro" of 1957 and the letters about it, especially his replies to Jean Malaquais to whom he dedicates *Barbary Shore* and whose Trotskyite influence is evident everywhere in it. In "Advertisements for Games and Ends," he asserts that "the white Protestant's ultimate sympathy must be with science, factology, and the committee rather than with sex, birth, heat, flesh, creation, the sweet and the funky—they must go with the Russians rather than the Hip, for the Soviet sense of science and formal procedure will be more attractive to them."[47] But it is probably in a seminal essay entitled "Catholic and Protestant" that the connection between the technological revolution, attacked in *Of a Fire on the Moon*, and the sexual revolution, attacked in *The Prisoner of Sex*, is most evident: "History was created by man's decision to conquer Nature, and the evolution of his institutions may have come out of the need to shape the body and the mind into proper parts of a social machine which could move into attack upon the mysteries and powers of his existence."[48]

This passage predicts that "social lust to make units of people" which, in *The Prisoner of Sex*, is "the measure of the Liberal technologist and the Left totalitarian," and it at the same time dimly outlines the portrait of Neil Armstrong in *Of a Fire on the Moon*: "And so Armstrong, sitting in the commander's seat, space suit on, helmet on, plugged into electrical and environmental umbilicals, is a man who is not only a machine himself in the links of these networks . . . but is also . . . a veritable high priest of the forces of society and scientific history . . . a general of the church of the forces of technology, for think not of the fifteen miles of wire in that small capsule, but of the vast multi-million-dollar technological bands which belt the very economy of the nation."[49] Implicit in all these passages is the justification for Mailer's ending *Why Are We in Vietnam?* with the mention of the "electrified mind" of D. J. and Tex Hyde (Dr. Jekyll and Mr. Hyde are one at last) and for his allegation in *The Armies of the Night* that "the authority has operated on their [the young hippies'] brain with commercials."[50] "Brain" and "mind" are singular by obvious intention. What began as an interest in the control and manipulation of groups of men in an

[47] *Advertisements for Myself*, p. 388.
[48] *Ibid.*, p. 427.
[49] *Of a Fire on the Moon*, pp. 182–83.
[50] *The Armies of the Night*, p. 84.

army composed to represent the different segments of American society gradually developed into a metaphor of "twentieth-century man" as a kind of tooled collective.

In one of his many attempts to define what he means by metaphor, Mailer has remarked that it "exists to contain contradictions,"[51] and this proves to be the case even when he uses a word like "collective," which would seem mostly negative in its implications. In fact, as we have seen, the idea of man as "collective" has as many positive implications under Mailer's auspices as it has negative ones under the auspices of the Wasp-technocrat-totalitarian-cancer spreaders. In the one case, man is an accumulation of potentialities which he can realize only through struggle, so that, as we learn from "The Metaphysics of the Belly," "if we wish to be more masculine we must first satisfy something feminine in ourselves," and "the reverse is also true";[52] in the other, the "collective" state is roughly equivalent to one-dimensionality. In this Mailer is closer to Renaissance humanism than to any contemporary trend, to "what a piece of work is a man," and he would come down positively on the implication of "work"—that manhood is a job to be done, not a product to be studied.

Though he famously claims that "one exists in the present, in that enormous present without past or future, memory or planned intention,"[53] Mailer is in fact rooted to a theological and literary humanistic heritage. He is an anticapitalistic, anti-industrial, antitechnological pastoralist, and among the books that might be sought out for some understanding of him are Tawney's *Religion and the Rise of Capitalism* as much as Wilhelm Reich's *The Function of the Orgasm*. He is dependent on a past which is essentially mythic and he prefers to think of a man, and of himself, as someone living within the perils of time while knowing that he is

[51] *Cannibals and Christians*, p. 340.
[52] *Ibid.*, p. 292.
[53] *Advertisements for Myself*, p. 339.

the carrier of life which is not wholly his own to waste. He is committed to the most primitive religious traditions; so much so that, despite his Roman Catholic inclinations on the subject of sex, he will not allow the sacrifice of Christ as a way of forgiving the sons for the sins of the fathers. Because of what he considers Christ's miscalculation, Mailer can even propose that "in the seed of Christianity was an origin of technology, and even conceivably an origin of human mediocrity."[54] Mailer has to look back somewhere beyond Christ, then, beyond the point in history where the measure of history changed, in order that he might "begin to believe . . . that the marrows and sinews of creation were locked in the roots of an amputated past."[55] These are presumably equivalent to the "hieroglyphics of the chromosome (so much like primitive writing)" which in *The Armies of the Night* are imagined as "that tissue of past history . . . being bombed by the use of LSD as outrageously as the atoll on Eniwetok, Hiroshima, Nagasaki, and the scorched foliage of Vietnam."[56] It doesn't matter that this might well serve as a Birchite answer to a hippie antiwar demonstration, since it is in the nature of such an argument as Mailer's to dismiss the local and the immediate in the interests of circumstances so largely conceived as to be outside history altogether.

Because of his radically conservative view of contemporary experience, it might be asked how he could ever have claimed to favor a sexual revolution. The "link"—such a favored word in Mailer—"between sexual repression and political repression" was noted in "The Homosexual Villain" in 1954, and along with it came the information that "a fascinating thesis on this subject is *The Sexual Revolution* by Wilhelm Reich."[57] Choosing to find antisexuality at the foundation of all

[54] *The Prisoner of Sex*, p. 186.
[55] *Ibid.*, p. 222.
[56] *The Armies of the Night*, p. 93.
[57] *Advertisements for Myself*, p. 225.

organized power in America, Mailer could at about the
same time, in 1956, claim in "A Public Notice for
Godot" that "the only revolution which will be meaningful and natural for the twentieth century will be a
sexual revolution," and he offers in evidence "the comic
feminization of what had once been the iron commissars
of the Soviet superstate."[58] Mailer's example is especially interesting because he will be at pains in *The
Prisoner of Sex* to associate advocates of Women's
Liberation, of the single sexual standard and of sexual
permissiveness, with Stalinism and hence with the
betrayal of revolution in this century. The tracts for
Women's Liberation are written, he complains, in a
"prose reminiscent of the worst of the old party line,"[59]
and Kate Millett, whom he calls comrade, "is not so
much Molotov as Vishinsky,"[60] the prosecutor at the
Moscow trials.

The odd fact of the matter is that while Mailer is
always advocating revolutions—of consciousness, of
minorities, of sexual radicals—no successful revolution
is possible within the terms he sets and none would be
temperamentally acceptable to him. He does not want
an accomplished revolution, assuming there even is such
a thing. Rather he wants the intensification of the dialectical tensions that induce revolutionary fervor. If he
ever achieved real power, he would, like Mao, bring
about the disruption of his own establishment. He
would subscribe, I suspect, to two speeches of August
1937 and February 1957 "On Contradiction" in which
Mao talks about "the movement of opposites in the
whole process of development," their "mutual transformation," and "the supersession of the old by the new"
as the result of the process. In Mailer, the "new"
becomes simply the radical restatement of the mythic

[58] *Ibid.*, p. 335.
[59] *The Prisoner of Sex*, p. 39.
[60] *Ibid.*, p. 148.

"old," especially in his imagination of masculinity and femininity.

The movement of opposites is permanently necessary to Mailer, and in his world the only real defeat is in any illusion of victory or of the self-sufficiency of one side of a dialectical opposition. In his superb discussion of Lawrence in *The Prisoner of Sex* he gives him a position he obviously covets for himself: he was "a great writer because he contained a cauldron of boiling opposites."[61] Mailer's claim to being a revolutionary is thus implicit in the contradictoriness of his self-designation as a Left conservative. Uneasy about the possible sentimental excesses of his position, he claims rather defensively in *The Prisoner of Sex* that "no matter how conservative he became . . . he was still a revolutionary, for conservatism had been destroyed by the corporations of the conservatives, their plastic, their advertising, their technology. . . . Their capture of the future would be a fascistic botch. . . . The world would seek solutions where technology was faith and you stayed inside the system."[62]

Mailer's style, especially in his fervid efforts to link together, even if in opposition, subjects that liberal or technocratic thinkers would like to keep systematically discrete, is a way of writing himself *out* of the going "system," especially as it structures itself in the language of the computer as illustrated in parts of *Why Are We in Vietnam?* and *Of a Fire on the Moon*. In fact, "only the Novelist," as Mailer idealizes the role, can now work "with emotions which are at the very edge of the word system, and so is out beyond the scientists, doctors, psychologists, even—if he is good enough—the best of his contemporaries who work at philosophy itself."[63]

While I am prepared to believe that this might be true in some case, it doesn't seem to me to be true for Mailer, or for anyone now writing novels. Just as, in spite of his

[61] *Ibid.*, p. 137.
[62] *Ibid.*, pp. 223–24.
[63] *Ibid.*, p. 124.

concern for "opposites," Mailer has become so mechanical and repetitious in his use of them as to be anything but "a cauldron of boiling opposites," a genius in the manner of Lawrence, so he does not yet fit the dimensions he gives here to "the Novelist." His very formulation is evidence enough of why he should not think of himself as belonging, in his explorations of language systems, with "the best of his contemporaries who work at philosophy." For it is not "the emotions . . . at the very edge of the word system" which are the challenge to be met, but rather the word system itself—including literature, of course—as a source and producer of those emotions.

Mailer is in fact the best example of what I mean. He is a victim of the word systems he has been creating since the mid-1950s. They increasingly dictate his feelings and his ideas, propelling him into such follies as his belief that natural contraception would take over once women were freed of all merely mechanical means of contraception, or his notion of the power of the female ovum to "call across the diminishing sea"[64] to a "Y" instead of an "X" chromosome, thereby making the ovum as important in the determination of the sex of the child as is the male sperm. An earlier and portentous example was in his stubborn insistence on demographic authentication of the existence of "white Negroes." Thus, when Jean Malaquais objected that Mailer had ignored the fact that the American hipster has an equivalent in countries where there is no Negro population and that therefore hipsterism cannot be explained by reference to Black styles, Mailer countered that the "Negro's experience appears to be the most universal communication of the West"[65] thanks to an international taste for Negro jazz.

Mailer can of course believe what he wants, including

[64] *Ibid.*, p. 131.
[65] *Advertisements for Myself*, p. 364.

that the sex of the child may be determined by the qualities called forth by the fuck, but such notions result not from working with language, not even from explorations of emotions that exist at the edge of the so-called "word system," but from what he more aptly calls "metaphysical drift,"[66] a drift which is at the same time buttressed by schoolboy citations of data which in some cases, as in the matter of the call from the ovum to the "Y" chromosome, he must later admit are the result merely of "technical ignorance."[67]

He is, I'm afraid, rather presumptuous in his Coleridgean concern about the possible damage to Inspiration and Imagination, as these are embodied in himself, because he lives in an age dominated by technology. For the Imagination does not become subservient to science or technology—that tired and shriveled chestnut heated over and overheated throughout Mailer's works—simply by anyone's informing himself of what science and technology propose as realities. Science and technology deserve title to the Imagination at least as much as literature does, and altogether more than anything called literature written since at least World War II. The one conspicuous frailty in Mailer's otherwise noble and free exposure of himself to the forces now at work in the shaping of life is his vulgar and easy opposition between himself as Novelist and technology or science as System.

It is this failing, more than male chauvinism, which makes *The Prisoner of Sex* such an interestingly flawed, exciting, and yet aggravating book. His chauvinism goes way beyond the war of the sexes. It becomes a war of worlds, and as the antagonist on the side of Imagination, as the hero-creator, it is necessary for him not so much to justify the masculine urge toward domination over women as to claim that he himself has to express this

[66] *The Prisoner of Sex*, p. 132.
[67] *Ibid.*, p. 207.

urge in his role as a Creator. That is why his long defenses in *The Prisoner of Sex* of fellow male artists— especially of Henry Miller and D. H. Lawrence—are an integral part of his argument about the nature of the sexes and about the masculine need to dominate a space corresponding to the inner space which is the womb, the true source of the future. As a novelist, Mailer imagines that he is both maker and gestator of an equivalent future, and it is not too much to say that when he imagines America at the end of *The Armies of the Night* as heavy with child, in a section called "The Metaphor Delivered," he is all things at once: the Imagination that has impregnated this "beauty of magnificence unparalleled, now a beauty with leprous skin," the beauty herself, and the child (or metaphor) which she (he) is to deliver. Like a metaphor, as Mailer conceives it, the child holds within itself possibilities that represent a dialectical contradiction—it may prove to be either "the most fearsome totalitarianism the world has ever known" or "a babe of a new world, brave and tender, artful and wild."[68]

I do not offer these remarks as an interpretation of the end of the book, nor do I mean them fancifully as applied to Mailer's imagination of himself as a writer. Rather, I am trying to reach again the buried sources of Mailer's power and of his extraordinary sense of the consequences to history of his investing that power in writing. In his imagined involvement with time—the past, present, future—he assumes all the roles in the procreative process and does so by virtue, as he sees it, of being the Novelist. The experiences in the present, for example, in the on-the-spot occurrences recorded in *The Armies of the Night* and *Miami and the Siege of Chicago*, the political and fight reporting in *The Presidential Papers* and *Cannibals and Christians*, the personal anecdotes in *Of a Fire on the Moon* and *The*

[68] *The Armies of the Night*, p. 288.

Prisoner of Sex (such as the nice bit about housekeeping at the beginning of the latter, and the wonderful story of burying the car which ends the former)—all have the same peculiarity, as we have seen, with respect to time. Because of that peculiarity, all can be called the work of a Novelist, in his sense of it, rather than of a journalist. As a man in time he is always being a Novelist with an eye to what he will make in the future. So that he has not only what he calls, in *The Prisoner of Sex*, "man's powerful sense of the present"; he can also claim to be like a woman who, he believes, contains "the future as well as the present" and as a result "has lived a physical life"—precisely where Mailer chooses to live his life as existentialist and writer—"on the edge of the divide."[69] If women can be considered a man's indispensable and only connection to the future, then writing can be considered for Mailer the exercise of a feminine attribute by a man who has already displayed a masculine capacity to live powerfully in a present which is to take a future and final form in his writing. I would guess that his choice of topics for that writing, being as they are invariably and conspicuously masculine, is a sort of anticipatory compensation for the feminine exercise of delivering these topics to the world.

It is perhaps possible now to see more clearly into what I have called Mailer's amnesia. Once he decided in his teens to become a writer, once he thought of the career of writing as his future, all of his present became his past. All the past, everything that existed before that point, was consigned to literary oblivion; he had not lived through it with the expectation that it was to be a part of the only future he was to know, his future as a writer. It is hard to imagine a more purely, more instinctively literary mind than his, to the degree even that it treats what is presently going on as if it were already memory, as if the present were always in some sense retrospec-

[69] *The Prisoner of Sex*, p. 60.

tive, as if in the present he projected himself to the future, there to look back on what is going on as if it were the past.

Given this special involvement with time, it is understandable that most of Mailer's experience is teleological and guilt-ridden, all of it infinitely subject to expansions and linkages of association and opposition. It is also understandable why he should have the sexual attitudes that have become increasingly more pronounced and biased. Putting the matter perhaps too bluntly, the connection between writing and time in Mailer is the same as the connection between fucking and creation, and I would not assume necessarily that the sexual sequence dictated the literary one. In all likelihood it works the other way round, or perhaps both sequences claim equal jurisdiction to the same psychic structure. Fucking takes place in the present, the orgasm is of the present, but it looks forward in two ways, assuming it freely and fully engages the body: to greater future orgasms—equivalent to the writing that will give birth to the Big Novel—and to the chance that this orgasm has initiated the creation of a child whose shape will emerge in the future—equivalent to any book that is the intended consequence of some present or local involvement. The present is always awaiting the future as a time when one can get to know and recognize the shape of what one has done in the past.

This means simply that no experience in Mailer is ever free, ever disconnected, ever unlinked. Everyone, and that includes the reader, is always made a "prisoner" in his work because it is impossible for him to imagine sex or any other human act which is not in the throes of dialectic. So great is his emphasis on the necessity to life of dialectical oppositions that after some acquaintance with his work it is easy to guess what his attitudes will be on any given subject. As an example, his comments on the relations of whites and Negroes in 1959, in the "Sixth Advertisement for Myself," are nearly identical with what he is to say over a decade later about the relations of another repressed group to a superior group, women to men, in *The Prisoner of Sex.* "The comedy is that the white loathes the idea of the Negro attaining equality in the classroom," he wrote in the first instance, "because the white feels that the Negro already enjoys sensual superiority. So the white unconsciously feels that the balance has been kept, that the old arrangement was fair. The Negro had his sexual supremacy and the white had his white supremacy."[70] Similarly, he argues in *The Prisoner of Sex* that the male desire for dominance is the desire not for tyranny but for equality. In their relation to time, to history, whether it be in writing or in other forms of action, all men, as Mailer sees them, are to a degree like Lawrence, for whom dominance "was the indispensable elevator which would raise his phallus to that height from which it might seek transcendence . . . some ecstasy where he could lose his ego for a moment."[71] Women, Mailer assures us, already have this sense of transcendence, traveling as they do "through the same variety of space" occupied by men but "in full possession of a mysterious space within."[72] No wonder women are already "on the edge of the divide" to which men like Mailer can arrive only after great struggle and where they must struggle still harder to maintain their equilibrium. "Women, like men, were human beings," he further assures us, "but they were a step, or a stage, or a move, or a leap nearer the creation of existence."[73]

The usefulness of such contentions to the conduct of life is where we find it, but the habit of mind, in this and in other crucial instances, is what primarily interests me. Mailer's resolute practice is to probe for a feeling of repression where there would for others be

[70] *Advertisements for Myself*, p. 332.
[71] *The Prisoner of Sex*, p. 155.
[72] *Ibid.*, p. 59.
[73] *Ibid.*, p. 60.

evidence only of the power of the oppressor, to find in the apparent majority the characteristics of a minority, and to cultivate in himself what might be called the minority within.

.

The Minority Within

iii

Like all his other theories, Mailer's theories about the relations between the sexes reveal his intuitive taste for "war," for the conflict by which one at last delineates the true form of oneself and of others. "War" is only an occasion, however, for his effort to discover the minority element within any person, constituency, or force which might be engaged in a "war." And it is this minority element which has the most beneficially corrosive effect upon form, forcing it to dispense with its merely acquired or protective or decorative attributes. It might be more accurate to say, in dealing with this very slippery subject, that "war" provides the context within which any creative minority pressure can assert itself formatively within society, the self, or a book.

This feature of Mailer is more complicated than one might infer from the sometimes simplified dichotomies in which he indulges. The minority element is not equivalent, that is, to one side in the "war," the dualisms or oppositions found everywhere in his work. The minority is not God or the Devil, Black or white, woman or man. Rather it is that element in each which has somehow been repressed or stifled by conformity to system—including systematic dialectical opposition—or by fear of some power, like death, which is altogether larger than the ostensible, necessarily more manageable opponent apparently assigned by history. The minority element in males or Blacks or God is the result of their inward sense of inferiority which the outward or visible opposition from women or whites or the Devil did not of itself necessarily create. Blacks do not feel inferior to whites so much as to the psychotic brilliance created and, at once, thwarted within themselves by the accident of white oppression; whites do not feel superior to Blacks but inwardly terrified at the possibility that in any open sexual competition they would prove inferior. Behind each of his dualisms, Mailer's imagination searches out, sometimes with a harried ingenuity, the minority incentive that in turn gives dialectical energy to the dualism.

His fascination for boxing is best understood in this way. Within the historically identified fights between Liston and Patterson, for example, Mailer postulates disguised feelings and minority forces which then allow him to redefine the fight as a metaphysical conflict. Two men trying to beat each other into unconsciousness are looking, as he reports in one of the best pieces of writing he has ever done, "The Eleventh Presidential Paper— Death," for some "half human way to kill a little in order not to deaden all" with an otherwise "frustrated and thus sickening need to suppress the violence that is an indispensable element of life."[1] But if boxing is "murder" it is still more secretly a form of love-making.

[1] *The Presidential Papers*, p. 247.

The boxing metaphors of his sexual descriptions are pro-
lific, even lurid, especially in "The Time of Her Time"
and in many casual references to himself, as when,
describing his conduct on a television show with Nelson
Algren, he says that he "was as mad as a lazybitch
boxer."[2] He proposes that one can like the sex in Henry
Miller's *Tropic of Cancer* the way one likes a club fight,[3]
and in *King of the Hill* he tells us that in training Ali
was "perfecting the essence of his art which was to make
the other fighter fall secretly, helpless in love with
him."[4] The ring is both an arena and a four-poster bed.

Because usually suppressed and unacknowledged,
these are finally the most energizing impulses within two
men who meet in the ring. The range of associations that
reach behind and beyond the visibly contending elements—in one direction toward sexual love and in the
other toward death—makes boxing a particularly good
example of what Mailer likes to do with the linked
oppositions he sets up. So much so that in a championship fight, not merely men but Beings and Universes
collide, "on an adventure whose end is unknown."[5] He
is therefore given license to move up and down the
linked oppositions at will, and can write of the outcome,
in this case a victory for Liston over Patterson:

> The world quivered in some rarified accounting of
> subtle psychic seismographs, and the stocks of certain
> ideal archtypes shifted their status in our country's
> brain. Sex had proved superior to Love still one more
> time, the Hustler had taken another pool game from
> the Infantryman, the Syndicate rolled out the Liberal,
> the Magician hyped the Artist, and since there were
> more than a few who insisted on seeing them simply
> as God and the Devil (whichever much or little of

---

[2] *Cannibals and Christians*, p. 177.
[3] *Ibid.*, p. 198.
[4] *King of the Hill*, pp. 54–55.
[5] *The Presidential Papers*, p. 255.

either they might be), then the Devil had shown that the Lord was dramatically weak.[6]

The war between God and the Devil figures in nearly everything Mailer has written, and in his theology a man's efforts can apparently help one side or the other. But even in each of these presumably ultimate opponents, Mailer finds a sense of minority status. God can fill man with fear, he allows in an exegesis of Martin Buber's *Tales of the Hasidim*, "but it is the profound fear God feels himself."[7] While God is afraid that the Devil may emerge victorious, still more terrifying to him is the possibility that either (or both) may fail, thereby dissipating the dialectical tensions that are as essential to God's as to the Devil's power. Each might exhaust the other, but both might be destroyed by "the plague." "Perhaps the Devil," as we are told in "The Political Economy of Time," "bears the same relation to the plague that Faust bears to Mephisto,"[8] and without the Devil there could be no God in Mailer's universe, only entropy. He is quite unable to imagine anything except in oppositions, unable even to imagine one side of the opposition without proposing that it has yet another opposition within itself. Thus, it is not merely dialectical oppositions which are essential to the activities and movements of Mailer's imagination but the further complication that there be within each side a sense of internal embattlement.

What appalls him about the technologizing of life is that it induces psychic pacification. It removes the awe one should feel about sex, dulls one's sense of death (and thereby of life) by the provision of palliatives, and can even lay claim to one of the principal literary terrains reserved to the imagination, and to death, which is the moon. "Technology," he suspects in *The Prisoner of*

---

[6] *Ibid.*
[7] *Cannibals and Christians*, p. 337.
[8] *Ibid.*, p. 364.

Sex, "was the assertion of men who were not notably gifted at arts of war and love,"[9] two activities, as he sees, them, which are productive of life or at least of the human struggle to define what is properly human. Mailer's sense of life has become nearly indistinguishable from his feeling for minority status. It is the last possible stay against uniformity and "cancer," by which he means the unopposed proliferation of undifferentiated cells.

Always linking rebelliousness or contention with creativity and love, he writes in "The White Negro" that cancer is "a slow death by conformity with every creative and rebellious instinct stifled."[10] Not to insist on the differentiation of the sexes in other than physiological ways, or to have a single standard for both, does more than remove the dialectical opposition between men and women. It constitutes a lie, as Mailer sees it, about the internal nature of both; it contravenes the evidence that from inception each of the sexes faces quite different challenges and has a separate program of development. The very effort of the sperm to enter the ovum is heroic enough, but Mailer wants to insist that the "Y" or male chromosome has an especially difficult time. Of the possible forty-six chromosomes that constitute the combined total from a sperm and an egg, the "Y" chromosome is a minority member because in the determination of sex the female can contribute an "X" but cannot contribute a "Y," the male an "X" or a "Y." Furthermore, Mailer is happy to cite Dr. Landrum B. Shettles, co-author of *Your Baby's Sex: Now You Can Choose*, to the effect that in any competition to reach, penetrate, and fertilize the ovum, the "Y" chromosome in the sperm is at a disadvantage when compared with the "X" chromosome in the same sperm. Whatever way you look at it, war *and* love are essential to the very beginning of form as represented by the human body,

[9] *The Prisoner of Sex*, p. 67.
[10] *Advertisements for Myself*, p. 339.

especially a male body. The male or "Y" chromosome is thus endowed in Mailer's account with characteristics of a heroically disadvantaged warrior:

> That "outer core," those external regions of the ovum which sperm must first penetrate, were, he must suppose, a cameo of the female, sensitive as any other female flesh to the presence of the man who would enter her.[11]

Mailer is not content to record the tribulations of the male chromosome or to suggest that its actions dramatize the necessity from the very outset of the masculine passion for self-definition. No, he is on the trail of bigger game. The male copulator is after all a product of the very drama for whose re-enactment he is in the process of making himself responsible. From his inception, that is, he was given a hint of the possible unworthiness of his efforts to penetrate female flesh. Hence he feels like a minority in the sack as well as in the vagina, hence, too, the inducement, the challenge, the primary excitation of possible exclusion. Mailer's interpretation of the male thrust toward domination shows, once again, how far back and into what regions beyond personal memory he will go to find a Past. All the more reason why he should feel that efforts truly to enter women are necessarily corrupted by technological or contraceptive interference; the sperm is curtailed of its own necessary urge, its need to go home again, not to the vagina or the womb, for such would be mere Freudian sentimentality, but to the very ovum. And imagine the trauma of sperm released in the rectum, where there is not even an ovum to meet it! Mailer "must suppose" this connection between the sperm's difficulty in penetrating the ovum and a woman's sensitive resistance (so instinctive it is really her very "flesh" which is "sensitive . . . to the presence of a man who would enter her"), because on

[11] *The Prisoner of Sex*, p. 207.

this supposition rests his entire argument against the sexual theory of Women's Liberation. Their elementary error is the assumption that it is they who have a minority status in their sexual commerce with men.

He would claim that it is really the male who feels inferior and who must therefore assume a corrective dominancy in social and sexual intercourse. Any woman who accepts her true status, her inward sense of prowess, can afford to allow the male his effort at an outward domination. After all, it merely brings him to a level of equality. It is characteristic of the flirtatiousness of this argument, which might work quite well enough in a fraternity-house seduction scene, that while Mailer talks about the "effort" and the "passion" necessary "to become a man" he suggests that it is no more easy "to agree to be a woman."[12] This is sophomoric trickery, since it is by nature altogether easier to "agree" to be something than to become something for which one has only the potentiality.

In Mailer, women really need to do little more than act like the niggers in Faulkner: they are "free," in Faulknerian rhetoric, when they simply endure, leaving the whites with the burden of injustice. Thus Sergius, in "The Time of Her Time," is allowed (with no hint of joking, I'm afraid) to say of Denise, when she loses the rhythm of a fuck, that "she had fled the domination which was liberty for her."[13] Sergius feels this way because he is hip, and it would not be unfair to assume that one reason he is hip is that the "Y" chromosome that produced him—indeed any "Y" chromosome, regardless of how its initial work is later thwarted—is also hip. This is pretty clearly suggested in a continuation of the passage already quoted from *The Prisoner of Sex*:

[12] *Ibid.*, p. 168.
[13] *Advertisements for Myself*, p. 490.

Indeed how could the sperm cell fail to force its way with different strength and rhythm if it were an x-bearing female cell, or a male y? The x cells were (as he had just learned) oval and large, the y were round and small. In fact beneath the light of the phase-contrast microscope, the female sperm cells showed themselves to be sturdy and the male cells quick: the female could survive for days in the Fallopian tubes until the egg was ready to ovulate, but the male cells did not live longer than twenty-four hours and also perished more quickly in the acids of the vagina; this had to imply that a male embryo was the product of timing and speed—only on the day of ovulation could you create a boy.[14]

If the "Y" chromosome, indeed if the sperm itself is Hip, then the ovum is relatively Square. And it is to the point that his reference in 1970 to the "cameo" of the female ovum reverberates from 1957. Describing the danger which is a part of the everyday experience of the Negro, he contrasts it to "the cameo of security for the average white: mother and the home, job and the family."[15]

Since about 1957 and "The White Negro," Mailer has come to associate creativity and the imagination with the assertion of a minority position, and his contempt for liberals is a consequence of his conviction that they would deprive us of the vicissitudes and oppositions which are the necessary conditions for art and for any full sense of life. In "The Tenth Presidential Paper —Minorities" he claims that

> Minority groups are the artistic nerves of the republic, and like any phenomenon which has to do with art, they are profoundly divided. They are both themselves and the mirror of their culture as it reacts upon them. They are themselves and the negative truth of themselves. No white man, for example, can hate the

[14] The Prisoner of Sex, pp. 207–208.
[15] Advertisements for Myself, p. 340.

Negro race with the same passionate hatred that each Negro feels for himself and for his people; no anti-Semite can begin to comprehend the malicious analysis of his soul which every Jew indulges every day.[16]

Still later, in "A Speech at Berkeley on Vietnam Day," he proposes that anyone in America, even the President, is "a member of a minority group if he contains two opposed notions of himself at the same time." He claims that

What characterizes the sensation of being a member of a minority group is that one's emotions are forever locked in the chains of ambivalence—the expression of an emotion forever releasing its opposite—the ego in perpetual transit from the tower to the dungeon and back again. By this definition nearly everyone in America is a member of a minority group, alienated from the self by a double sense of identity and so at the mercy of a self which demands action and more action to define the most rudimentary borders of identity.[17]

Such passages indicate why Mailer is a more difficult writer in a book like *An American Dream* or in *Why Are We in Vietnam?* than most critics or reviewers are prepared to recognize. Not everyone is qualified for the kind of reading, the reading as much with the ear as with the eye, that his writing calls for; not everyone is capable of caring for the drama of his argument and of his language, as it plays across the page; and very few are prepared for his unique mixtures of the world of daily news, the world we take for granted, with the world of nightmare and psychotic imagining. He is now quite unlike any other writer of his generation. He is more like Pynchon than, say, like Burroughs (or Borges), with whom he has similarities enough to make the differences instructive. Burroughs is interested in

---

[16] *The Presidential Papers*, p. 187.
[17] *Cannibals and Christians*, p. 77.

showing how the world of the underground is a metaphor for the world we all live in, while Mailer insists on the fact that the world we live in *is* the underground. And Borges, for all his marvelous facility and wit, becomes, after any extended reading, tedious and emasculating. He is forever demonstrating the fictive nature of reality, forever calling us away from the dangers of contemporary facts, Argentinian or otherwise, to the refuge of fable-izing and the titillation of literary bewilderment. Burroughs is a writer of genius comparable to Mailer's and essential to the latter's development, especially in *Why Are We in Vietnam?*, but the currently touted Borges is the kind of writer whose relation to the possibilities of literature is like the relation of a good cookbook to food.

Mailer insists on living *at* the divide, living *on* the divide, between the world of recorded reality and a world of omens, spirits, and powers, only that his presence there may blur the distinction. He seals and obliterates the gap he finds, like a sacrificial warrior or, as he would probably prefer, like a Christ who brings not peace but a sword, not forgiveness for past sins but an example of the pains necessary to secure a future. This fusion in the self of conflicting realms makes him a disturbing, a difficult, and an important writer. I use these terms deliberately, to suggest that his willingness to remain locked into "the chains of ambivalence" is a measure of the dimension and immediacy of his concerns, of his willingness not to foreclose on his material in the interests of merely formal resolutions. There is no satisfactory form for his imagination when it is most alive. There are only exercises for it. Of course any particular exercise can in the long run become equivalent to a form, and when that happens Mailer is least interesting to himself or to us, as in those parts in *Of a Fire on the Moon* that boringly reduce everything to favorite categories, or in some of his extended demonstrations of what a smart boy he can be in his self-interviews.

Why Are We in Vietnam? and *The Armies of the Night*, along with parts of *Advertisements for Myself* and *An American Dream*, make Mailer easily the equal, it seems to me, of Fitzgerald and Hemingway, potentially of Faulkner. His accomplishment deserves comparison with theirs precisely because it is of a different kind and because it takes account of the varieties, evolutions, discontinuities, and accumulations of style since World War II. But he could not be to our time what they were to theirs without being in many important respects radically unlike them in the way he writes. No other American writer of this period has tried so resolutely and so successfully to account for the eclecticisms of contemporary life when it comes to ideas of form, of language, of culture, of political and social structures, and of the self.

The reason why most thoughtful and literate young readers prefer Mailer to, say, Updike or Roth or Malamud is that his timing is synchronized to theirs, while the others move to an older beat. Which is to say something not only about Mailer's taste for certain situations but also about a taste for Mailer, for the pace and movement of his writing. I suspect that an enthusiasm for his work means that one shares his partiality for those moments where more is happening than one can very easily assimilate. By and large, the other contemporary writers I have mentioned will not allow more to happen than can be accounted for in the forms they have settled upon. They work away from rather than into the ultimate inconsistencies, the central incoherence in the way we live now. Mailer, on the other hand, is always looking for the stylistic equivalent for that movement of "the ego in perpetual transit from tower to dungeon and back again."

It is no accident that *An American Dream*, which incidentally seems to move rather frequently between the Waldorf Towers and police headquarters, finds its most appreciative audience among serious young students of literature who have a surer instinct for what it offers than have most of Mailer's critics. The always outmoded criteria of verisimilitude, the accusations that the characterization of Rojack is the occasion merely for a vulgar ego trip by Mailer, the charge that the book is simply dirty and that it fails for not making the hero pay for the crime of murder—these allegations sound primitive enough for hill-country journalism of a bygone era, but they happen to have been sponsored by, among others, Philip Rahv, Elizabeth Hardwick, and Tom Wolfe, who complains of "unreal dialogue" as if there were such a thing as "real" dialogue. Even to evoke criteria of this kind betrays an inability to see what the book is about, and I mention these criticisms only because they represent the persistence of standards—and there are of course many young pseudoneoclassicists coming through the ranks—which continue to keep discussions of Mailer at an irrelevant and demeaning level even when some sympathetic critics set about to defend him.

Oddly enough, it is just because it *does* call for the kind of negative response it has mostly gotten that *An American Dream* is such a brilliant achievement. From the first sentence the novel lays a proprietary claim on the so-called real world, and even Tom Wolfe ought to have found the dialogue of the police or of a Mafia don, like Gannuchi, "real" enough. Within a couple of paragraphs we learn that Rojack went to Harvard (so did Mailer); that Rojack met Kennedy (Mailer did, too, though under quite different circumstances); that Rojack ran for Congress and won (while Mailer's first effort to run for Mayor of New York had already floundered); that Rojack killed his wife (Mailer had recently stabbed his second). Both were for a time held by the police; they are roughly the same age, Rojack, forty-four, and Mailer, at the time of writing, forty-one; Rojack is half and Mailer all Jewish; and both pursue the same topic—as writers and television personalities—

actions with Deborah's German maid, Ruta, just after the murder.

Rojack raises a most interesting question about Mailer. Even to arrive at that question, consider, first of all, that Rojack's efforts at self-creation in language are analogous to his efforts in action in that both are an attempt to discover the shape of his true self by daring each side of the divide on which he chooses to live. Consider further that his verbal transits between worlds are equivalent to Mailer's own movements up and down between the linked oppositions which hold so much of his work and of his world together. The question, then, is this: What does Rojack's condition, once he has escaped from this "perpetual transit," tell us about the kinds of fulfillment that Mailer wishes to arrive at as a writer? In order to be a writer at all, in order quite literally to write, it is perhaps necessary that he remain the embattled embodiment of the two worlds from which, in the hope of becoming a new man, in the hope of having a second birth, Rojack wants desperately to escape. Rojack wants to escape from the world as it is contrived and structured by conspiracies of power.

What is not sufficiently clarified, even by admirers of *An American Dream*—and I am thinking of two astute critics, Leo Bersani and Tony Tanner—is that Rojack really hopes to do more than that. He would also like to escape from his own, which is to say from Mailer's counterconspiracies, his alternative but often insane inventions. Above all, he would be "free of magic," not only the "magic at the top," that cluster of the incorporated social-economic-political power which Kelly seems to offer him as a bribe, but also the magic he evokes in order not to be tempted by the bribe. He wants to be free of the enslavement to system that is implicit in the total absorption of his opposition to system. Stepping out of the dialectical frame so nearly compulsive in Mailer, Rojack is allowed to say that he would like to escape "the tongue of the Devil, the dread of the Lord, I wanted to be some sort of rational man again, nailed tight to details, promiscuous, reasonable, blind to the reach of the seas."[19] His prayer simply is that he be allowed to "love that girl, and become a father, and try to be a good man, and do some decent work."[20] At last, with admiration, almost with relief, the reader can welcome back that modest, nice, young Jewish boy in Mailer who won't ever, quite, let himself be forgotten. If Rojack passes over a terrain already thoroughly explored by his creator, he reveals the otherwise scarcely articulated wish of his creator to arrive back home, where it all began.

Mailer's articulate brilliance depends on his not succeeding as a writer in a way Rojack proposes to succeed as a man. Perhaps for that reason Rojack cannot be allowed any palpable equivalence to his own language of love, to the nearly hippie simplicity with which he would replace his Hip embattlement. Rojack's feeling of possible mutation, as if "I had crossed a chasm of time and was some new breed of man,"[21] which occurs fairly early in the book, has only a grotesque realization at the end when, in Las Vegas to gamble for his trip onward alone to Guatemala and Yucatán—striking out like the classic American hero to the territory always beyond—he says, "Nobody knew that the deserts of the West, the arid empty wild blind deserts, were producing again a new breed of man."[22] However "new," this breed is, like the old one, suspended between two worlds: the one a horror of nature, "the bellows of the desert," the other of technology, the air-conditioned hotel where he spends twenty-three of every twenty-four hours as if "in a pleasure chamber of an encampment on the moon."[23]

The movement from the desert of this book to the icy

[19] *Ibid.*, p. 255.
[20] *Ibid.*, p. 162.
[21] *Ibid.*, p. 81.
[22] *Ibid.*, p. 268.
[23] *Loc. cit.*

North range of *Why Are We in Vietnam?* and then to the magnificently described craters of the moon in *Of a Fire on the Moon* may be Mailer's way of suggesting that because we have denuded and corrupted nature in those parts of our world where it might be hospitable, we are perforce engaging ourselves, by an urgency of the will akin to Sergeant Croft's in his assault on Mount Anaka, with those sanctuaries of nature which are least hospitable. And there we absorb the savagery and the urge to kill which is part of nature, while at the same time we accept the protections afforded by a wholly technological atmosphere unnatural to the environment in which it has been placed. Mailer thus proposes an insoluble paradox: that human savagery increases in direct proportion to our monumental achievements in those realms of technology which now imperially reach into the very last recesses of the natural world.

Mailer has come to posit situations in which the imaginable alternatives seem to be suicide or "a slow death by conformity, with every creative and rebellious instinct stifled."[24] For a man to operate on the "edge" of such a divide, facing two unacceptable invitations, is less humanly fulfilling, even, than for him to choose, say, to knock another man out in the ring. So that while Mailer concedes that boxing may not be a civilized activity, he can insist, rightly, I think, and even after witnessing the killing of Benny Peret, that "it belonged to the tradition of the humanist; it was a human activity, it showed part of what a man was like, it belonged to his ability to create art and artful movement on the edge of death or pain or danger or attack, and it had much to say about the subtleties of human style."[25]

The question being asked in all of his books from *An American Dream* to the present is, for him, steadfastly grim: Am I, Norman Mailer, at last an expendable

[24] *Advertisements for Myself*, p. 339.
[25] *The Presidential Papers*, p. 247.

human type, and is the "ability to create art" (which, again, ought not to be confused with the ability to absorb it or revere it as Culture) finally not simply irrelevant but perhaps actually a quixotic imposition that further exhausts the spirit of the writer and reader alike? Hints of exhaustion are evident, I fear, in *Of a Fire on the Moon* and *The Prisoner of Sex*. In these, more simply than in any other of his recent work, Mailer seems, in a crotchety and sentimental, an aggressively petulant and self-pitying way, to encamp himself as a Defender of the Imagination in an Age of Technology. Perhaps this explains, again, why some of the best parts of both books are about other artists and writers, other "defenders" of the faith, as in the exquisite discussions of Cézanne and Magritte in the moon book.

Where he has faced the question of creative impotence less explicitly, where he seems rather to get entangled with it against his will, he reveals something even more profitable to his writing than are his admirations for other artists, however much they reassure him that it is still possible, in Empson's phrase, to learn a style from a despair. I am referring to the passionate energy with which he displays his mastery, perhaps unequaled since the parodic brilliance of Joyce in *Ulysses*, of those expressive modes which threaten to obliterate his own expression, those contemporary styles that provide us too abundantly with images of what we possibly are in our public and in our private selves. He can do this while simultaneously demonstrating the greater inventiveness, inclusiveness, plasticity, and range of his own modes. Nowhere is this more impressively evident than in the most dazzling and the most incomprehensibly slighted of his novels, *Why Are We in Vietnam?*

The novel's answer to the question raised in its title fits none of the schemes of cause and effect that dominate nearly all "responsible" social and political thinking. And "responsible" it has proved to be—for the war. Vietnam is mentioned once, and then only in the last sentence. Instead Mailer is attempting, with a vitality akin to the Circe episode in *Ulysses*, to register the fevered mentality of which this atrocity is not so much a consequence as a part—so naturally a part that no one in the book needs consciously to be aware of the existence of Vietnam as in any way unique. It is not especially worth mentioning. We are in Vietnam because we are as we corporately are. We are all of one another. And for that reason Mailer makes the voices that speak to us in the book, in its various Intro Beeps, and Chaps, a matter of serious but comic bewilderment. Perhaps, as it mostly seems, what we get are emissions from the hopped-up mind of D. J., a Dallas late-adolescent son of corporation millionaire Rusty and of his wife, Hallie Lee Jethroe. We can't be sure. In this work D. J. functions as Mailer has done in others: as the theorist of multiple identity. He cautions us that

> we have no material physical site or locus for this record, because I can be in the act of writing it, recording it, slipping it (all unwitting to myself) into the transistorized electronic aisles and microfilm of the electronic Lord (who, if he is located in the asshole, must be Satan) or I can be an expiring consciousness, I can be the unwinding and unravelings of a nervous constellation just now executed, killed, severed or stopped, maybe even stunned, you thunders, Herman Melville go hump Moby and wash his Dick. Or maybe I am like a Spade and writing like a Shade.[26]

The "voice" here is a composite of styles, tones, and allusions transposed to the pace of a disc jockey's taped talk. Throughout the book this voice manages to incorporate nearly every kind of cant one can hear on the airways of America. To a lesser degree Rojack was also an assemblage of parts, some of them disjunctive with others. The often abrupt but deftly managed shifts of his style are one indication of this. (So, too, with Cherry.

[26] *Why Are We in Vietnam?*, p. 26.

Watching her sing under the spotlight in a nightclub, Rojack imagines that "she could have been a nest of separate personalities,"[27] a nice formula for his own and for Mailer's willing if more warlike gathering of disparate selves.)

Mailer's healthy and at last dogged refusal to put together a self at the cost of stifling any fragment of his personality enters into what can be called his willingness to decharacterize the people he likes. While giving full expression to the social and psychological identities which could be conventionally assigned to such characters, he proposes at the same time that they are impersonal units of energy, connected to powers quite unlike those which can account for a character in his other, more normal existence. This is why Mailer's heroes and heroines, especially in *An American Dream*, are a kind of battleground where external forces which inhabit the soul or the psyche war for possession. While Mailer admires the strength in a person like Rojack or Cherry that allows such a war even to go on, he also shares the terror they necessarily feel. In *An American Dream* and still more in *Why Are We in Vietnam?* is the acknowledgment that perhaps it is impossible to fashion any self that one can call one's own. Perhaps—and here the increasing influence of Burroughs on Mailer is apparent —we are no more than interchangeable, tooled parts of one another. D. J. is all he says he is and more, while American literature in the person of Herman Melville offers, at one point, a convenient scenario for the hunt in Alaska and, at another, the occasion only for a smart-ass joke.

D. J. is a character some of the time—a wild, brilliant, witty, savage, eager, and not unappealing boy; but he is much more than a character. He is the place, the context, the locus for an American mixture which is finally committed to the kill, and Melville is but one

[27] *An American Dream*, p. 97.

ingredient in the whipped-up, heated, soured mixture. The war already existed in that complex of pressures which shaped D. J. and the character of the nation and thus its fate, the "subtle oppression," as he describes it in *The Armies of the Night*, "which had come to America out of the very air of the century (this evil twentieth century with its curse on the species, its oppressive Faustian lusts, its technological excrement all over the conduits of nature, its entrapment of the innocence of the best)."[28] Vietnam, that is, did not induce this novel, but was itself induced by what the novel manages to gather up and redefine from everything Mailer had been saying for fifteen years or more about his country. And, as we are seeing, what he has to say about America is more than usually dependent upon what American literature has been saying for some one hundred and fifty years.

At a pace that is likely to overwhelm many readers, Mailer demonstrates his stylistic capacity to match the tempo of historical accelerations toward disaster. But he had already described that movement in the quieter tones of earlier work. It is consistent with what the novel is saying that he should have said much of it before—that it was there to be noted—in other, less compelling forms. As early as 1959 he offered a kind of prediction of the novel in "From Surplus Value to Mass Media," an essay which he calls "one of the most important short pieces" appearing in *Advertisements for Myself*. He proposed that if any new revolutionary vision of society is to be "captured by any of us in work or works," the necessary exploration will go

> not nearly so far into that jungle of political economy which Marx charted and so opened to rapid development, but rather will engage the empty words, dead themes, and sentimental voids of that mass media whose internal contradictions twist and quarter us be-

[28] *The Armies of the Night*, p. 114.

tween the lust of the economy (which radiates a greed to consume into us, with sex as the invisible salesman) and the guilt of the economy which must chill us with authority, charities for cancer, and all reminder that the mass consumer is only on drunken furlough from the ordering disciplines of church, F.B.I., and war.[29]

This passage proves particularly apt to *Why Are We in Vietnam?* The style of the novel is mimetic of the arts of the absurd he finds so chilling in a prefatory note to *Cannibals and Christians*, "Our Argument Fully Resumed." He there contrasts the art of self-expression (for which he offers the quite peculiarly inappropriate examples of Joyce and Picasso) which came out of the nineteenth century of iron frustration, with the arts which evolved after World War II, when children "grew up not on frustration but interruption." This later art is designed to shatter the nerves with "style, with wit, each explosion a guide to building a new nervous system." Dealing with "categories and hierarchies of discontinuity and the style of their breaks," it goes out to "hustle fifty themes in an hour."[30] It is an art which mass produces the wastes of art, though he doesn't quite get around to being that explicit about it. As usual, he is not anxious to appear a defender of high culture even when his own logic directs him that way.

Why Are We in Vietnam? is a medley of "empty words" and "dead themes," and Mailer would appear to suggest that these are really the inventions of the mass media. In fact, they represent what the mass media has made out of high culture, of psychoanalysis, of literary criticism, of myth, and of Mailer's own favorite theological evocations, such as "dread." What lays waste to the human mind is a central subject of this novel. But that is to put the matter rather too simply. Still more important in understanding its rapid shifts of style is Mailer's preoccupation with the processes by which the mind is encouraged to turn its own contents, turn itself even, into waste.

This is of course a complicated process. It is dramatized in this novel by a remarkable combination of quick changes and constant repetitions. We find ourselves transported with almost maddening speed from one context to another, while we are forced to absorb along the way an insistent recurrence of phrases, names, allusions, actions, tones of voice. In other words, the constant interruptions which create such a variety of contexts and moods in the book make its structure analogous to the structure, as Mailer has defined it, of contemporary daily life. Whether digested or not, one momentary accumulation of meaning has to be flushed out to make room for the rapid infusion of the next. No word, no name, no allusion, no idea can rest for even a moment in the mood which it is supposed to secure, and so the book proliferates in interruptions which involve the splitting even of titles, like "Moby" and "Dick," and in puns that mock the very authority which licenses them: "But rest for the inst," D. J. tells the reader. The phrase creates a paradox by calling for a rest in a contraction so hurried as to suggest there can be none, and then continues—"Return to civ, which is to say syphilization and fuck James Joyce."[31]

There is no consciousness in the book wherein the reader is allowed to find any security, which is again a reminder of Joyce's *Ulysses* and of the disturbance felt by critics whenever they are confronted with this kind of phenomenon. Their tendency is then to invent now one now another schematization in which to garage their minds. Efforts to locate some source of authority in Mailer's novels reveal only that there is none. This is

[31] *Why Are We in Vietnam?*, p. 149.

as it must be, since his intent is to refer us to determinants in American life that are mysterious and unlocatable, and the more powerful for being so. The question addressed by the book is no longer the Marxist one of the exploitation of working time or even of the human sense of time by the profit motive. Rather, the question is the domination of pleasure and of inner time. Remember that in "From Surplus Value to Mass Media," Mailer takes the Marcusean view, without the Marcusean heaviness, that we are "only on drunken furlough from the ordering disciplines of church, F. B. I. and war." The appropriateness of these terms to the novel is evident: the two boys are, in effect, on furlough from the war, the book being a record of what presumably is passing through the head of D. J. as he and Tex sit at their farewell dinner in Dallas. More than that, no one in the novel is ever seen at work, except possibly Hallie's psychoanalyst, Leonard Levin Ficthe Rothenberg, alternately called Linnit Live'n Fixit Rottenbug or Dr. Fink Lenin Rodzianko. It can be said that the book is given wholly to interruptions and distractions, though there is no telling from what, unless it be the urge to kill or hump. This is true even for that part of the hunt in Alaska which is called a "purification ceremony" for the boys.

In a book so pointedly evasive about assigning responsibility for its voices, its shifts and modulations, it is all the more curious that the section in which this "rite" occurs gives evidence of a more total engagement of Mailer's genius than can be found in any other of his works except for *The Armies of the Night*, written in the next year. The section, from Chapter 8 to the end, making up nearly half the book, covers some of the Alaska safari organized by Rusty Jethroe for the Medium Assholes, as D. J. calls them, of his corporation—Rusty himself being a High Asshole—D. J., Tex, and the guide, Big Luke Fellinka, and it includes all the episodes in which the boys separate themselves from the other hunters, leave their weapons behind, and head north into the icy peaks of the Brooks Range. Their quite conscious ambition to "get the fear, shit, disgust and mixed shit tapeworm out of fucked up guts and overcharged nerves"[32] and to cleanse themselves of the "specific mix of mixed old shit"[33] represented by the talk and the tactics of their companions. These latter, though overarmed and assisted by a helicopter in their search for bear, still have to lie about their credit for the kill, as does D. J.'s father at the expense of his son. They are, as Tony Tanner points out in *The City of Words*, which includes one of the best essays written about Mailer, going "as far into the northern snow as they can, not to kill but to open themselves up to the mystery and dread of this geographical extreme."[34] Tanner connects this not only to Rojack's position on the parapet but to Mailer's position as a writer who tries "to keep an equilibrium on the 'dangerous edge of things' through the resources of his own style."[35]

This is of course a position not unfamiliar to American writers, and especially to Melville. There are Melvillean touches from the beginning of his work, as in the notation that Lieutenant Hearn in *The Naked and the Dead* wrote a college honors thesis on "A Study of the Cosmic Urge of Herman Melville"; he is an appropriately felt presence throughout Mailer's accounts of the voyage to the moon, and the character of Rojack has interesting similarities to Ahab. Both men are convinced of the presence of what Ahab calls "malicious agencies," both have been mutilated by them, both are demonic and opposed to demons, both make use of the mechanisms of capitalistic culture in an effort to reach a reality which that culture has not yet been able to assimilate, both are at once charismatic and repel-

[32] *Ibid.*, p. 176.
[33] *Ibid.*, p. 204.
[34] *The City of Words: American Fiction, 1950–1970*, p. 371.
[35] *Ibid.*, p. 371.

lent, both share a peculiar, manic belief in their powers to exhale influences on others—Rojack by shooting his psychic pellets at obnoxious people in a New York bar, and Ahab in his claims, at one point, that "Something shot from my dilated nostrils, he has inhaled it in his lungs. Starbuck now is mine"[36]—and both have a longing for the ordinary life which is denied them by the very nature of their heroic exertions. Above all, neither imagines that if nature is some alternative to society it is necessarily a benign one. Rojack does not assume that the craters of the moon are hospitable, and Mailer, gazing at moon rock, feels an affection that is also spooky. In Mailer's work, as far back as his first novel, man in nature is what Lawrence said Deerslayer truly proved to be: "isolate and a killer." In *Why Are We in Vietnam?* what is finally bequeathed by the presiding spirit of the North is the order to go forth and kill.

The important issue is not the identification, not even the uses made of other writers in a book like this, be they Melville or Faulkner or Lawrence. What should concern us, rather, is the necessity to bother with literature at all, within a complex of competing, equally urgent, or equally innocuous references. This novel tends to remind us of literature, to remind us that it is literature we are reading. But the literature which gets to us in this book has passed through other media which rend and shred it. Appropriately we are made to think of the diminishing claims of literature, its problematic existence in a book where all forms of expression and of consciousness are made problematic. The references to Melville and the "Dick" of "Moby" are on the same page as are other equally possible and proposed models for the narrative voice: movie-cutie George Hamilton, or a choice proposed in saying that "I'm coming on like Holden Caulfield when I'm really Dr. Jekyll with balls."

What I mean to suggest is that the trip by the boys

[36] Herman Melville, *Moby Dick* (Modern Library Edition, New York), p. 163.

alone into the wilderness, their trip to the "edge," is not quite in the same category as Rojack's imaginary and real extensions of his own power into equally perilous circumstances. Mailer's account of the trip reveals, more than does anything in his other books, a willingness to gamble imaginatively up to the limits of his *own* resources. The trip by the boys is made into an existential experience. But who could doubt that it would be? What is more interesting is that it is also, and emphatically, a literary one, with admixtures of film idols, fashionable intellectual guides like Marshall McLuhan, crossings of Shakespeare with Batman, of Katherine Anne Porter with Clare Boothe Luce. I don't mean that such a cheery and utilitarian treatment of literature is designed merely to characterize the boys and elicit our sad and amused contempt. Actually, the boys are made as bright as any potential reader, certainly as bright as most literary-academic ones. (After all, D. J. has ready access to his "Literary Handbook Metaphor Manual."[37] Their literary self-consciousness, combined with their intellectual savvy, is what enriches the episode of their excursion beyond anything like it in American literature since *The Adventures of Huckleberry Finn*, an earlier book "written" by an adolescent who, though he tried to avoid the "style" of his times as energetically as D. J. tries to imitate his, was nonetheless also its victim.

While D. J. and Tex can be compared respectively to Huck and Tom, they are both more like Tom to the degree that they eagerly subscribe to system, to doing things "by the book," though now "the book" encompasses film, TV, and disc jockeys. So much so that in important respects they do not exist as characters at all but as expressive filaments of some computerized mind. This is made especially important, for any understanding of what Mailer is up to, by the sudden attention given in Chap 10 to the phrase "purification ceremony."

[37] *Why Are We in Vietnam?*, p. 165.

They have not cleaned the pipes, not yet. They are still full of toilet plunger holes seen in caribou, and shattered guts and strewn-out souls of slaughtered game meats all over the Alaska air and Tex feels like he's never going to hunt again which is not unhorrendous for him since he's natural hunter, but then with one lightning leap from the button on his genius belt to the base of his brain-pan he gets the purification ceremony straight in his head, and announces to D. J. that they gonna wrap their weapons and lash them in a tree. . . .[38]

Clearly, the "ceremony" is something out of the "Literary Handbook Metaphor Manual," electronically banked and awaiting the proper signal. Just as obviously, the phrase is meant to trigger in the reader's mind some recollection of the "relinquishment" scene of Isaac McCaslin in Faulkner's "The Bear." The difference is that in Mailer's book the "ceremony" is as much a literary-critical exercise as it is an existential act, at least insofar as D. J. chooses to recollect it. If "the purification ceremony" exists as something one can get "straight in his head," then this alone is symptomatic of how even the effort to free oneself of waste is construed in this book as an act that partakes of that waste, that belongs, like so much else, to cultural and literary cliché.

Nor are these corrosive implications extemporized for this specific occasion only. From nearly the beginning, the trek North by the boys has been treated as something predigested. Included in the report of the experience is the kind of literary interpretation usually left to the ingenuity of academic close reading. The zest for the adventure is equaled, probably excelled, by D. J.'s zest for the literary analysis of it, along with instructions on how, when, and where to pay the needed kind of attention:

[38] *Ibid.*, p. 175.

. . . what they see is a range of mountains ahead with real peaks, and they are going to go on up into them. (Ice needle peaks are crystals to capture the messages of the world.)

There! You all posed y'all ready for the next adventure in the heartland of the North, well hold your piss, Sis, we're about to embark with Tex Hyde who is, insist upon it, a most peculiar blendaroon of humanity and evil, technological know-how, pure savagery, sweet aching secret American youth, and sheer downright meanness as well as genius instincts for occult power (he's just the type to whip asses at the Black Masses) as well as being crack athlete. Such consummate bundle of high contradictions talks naturally in a flat mean ass little voice. Better hear it.[39]

Some measure of the brilliance of Mailer's achievement in *Why Are We in Vietnam?* is that he makes us almost regret that it is such a funny book, among the comic masterpieces of American literature. It is a book that makes us yearn for what it disposes of in its jokes. It induces the wish that it were possible still to restore sincerity to the noble effort of a line of heroes stretching back from Faulkner to Emerson and Cooper: the trek to the "edge" of civilization, there to be cleansed of its contaminations.

In its honesty, however, the novel is even more pessimistic about such a gesture than is the interestingly related example of *St. Mawr.* Lawrence's landscape in that work is as savage and nonhuman in its beauty as is Mailer's. But while the literary pretension implicit in trying to take some encouragement from this landscape is sufficiently noted, the illusion that one can find there a clue to human transformation is nonetheless treated with an at least grim elation. Lawrence is able to elude the ironies of the situation much more directly than

[39] *Ibid.*, p. 162.

Mailer can: he rather bluntly asserts that however ludicrous the form of self-cleansing may be in this particular instance, it can still represent some more general and laudable possibilities of reawakening and renewal. "Man has to rouse himself afresh," he editorializes, "to cleanse the new accumulations of refuse. To win from the crude wild nature the victory and the power to make another start, and to cleanse behind him the century-deep deposits of layer upon layer of refuse."

Lawrence is not at all reticent about using Lou Witt's naïveté as sufficient cause for a large exhortation about "man"; Mailer refuses to arrange any comparable license for himself. D. J. has been allowed effectively to claim that he is the spokesman (which also means victim) of the electrified "mind" that takes us to Vietnam. He represents the oversoul as Univac. Since Mailer's purpose is to lend authority to the claim that D. J. has incorporated the "mind" of a historical moment, he cannot for that very reason promote an alternative voice capable of redemptive flourishes. He has already sacrificed to D. J.'s satirization the large rhetoric which Lawrence keeps as a privilege. All he can do is try to locate in D. J. some faint, some submerged minority life left behind, as it were, from the washed-out wastes of the humanistic tradition.

Mailer pushes his luck in this novel about as far as a writer can. He creates a consciousness which is disarmingly bright, funny, weirdly attractive, if one thinks of it in terms of "character," while simultaneously making it a kind of computer bank in which is stored the fragmented consciousness of everyone else in the book. In this role D. J. is not so much a character as the medium through which passes the hundreds of identifiable voices that circulate in the nation (and in our literature) and whose final message, ending the book, is "Vietnam, hot damn."[40]

[40] *Ibid.*, p. 208.

Except for one crucial talent, as we shall see, Mailer surrenders nearly everything to the consciousness identified as D. J. He allows it to desiccate his sense of continuity with the literature of the past. He puts his own sincerities up for parody, as in D. J.'s reference to "the Awe-Dread Bombardment from Mr. Sender"[41] and his marvelous contrast between "love" (which is "dialectic, man, back and forth, hate and sweet, leer-love, spit-tickle, bite-lick") and "corporation" (which is "DC, direct current, diehard charge, no dialectic man, just one-way street, they don't call it Washington, D. C., for nothing").[42] And he allows parody of himself, familiar enough in his self-interviews, to be joined to the parody of older literature, as when he refers to "shit," "Awe," and "Dread" as "that troika—that Cannibal Emperor of Nature's Psyche (this is D. J. being pontiferous, for we are contemplating emotion recollected in tranquillity back at the Dallas ass manse, RTPY—Remembrance Things Past, Yeah, you remember?"[43]

This passage points to perhaps the most significant way in which D. J. usurps the place Mailer usually reserves for himself. D. J. is allowed to operate narratively in Mailer's own most effective mode, the one which tells us most about his peculiar relationship to the passage of time. Everything in the Chaps is reported from memory, no matter how much it seems of the present, except for the occasional notice given to the dinner party at which all the material issues from the mind of D. J. The Intro Beeps continually alert us to this: "Repeat, all you deficient heads out there and nascent electronic gropers, memory is the seed of narrative, yeah, and D. J. grassed out at a formal dinner in his momma daddy's Dallas house with Tex in white smoking jacket across the table has brought back gobs

[41] *Ibid.*, p. 188.
[42] *Ibid.*, p. 126.
[43] *Ibid.*, pp. 186–87.

of Alaska hunt memory two years before."[44] Or, in another example, which includes an allusion to the very pertinent "Le bateau ivre" of Rimbaud and suggests also that D. J. has laid claim even to some of Mailer's Jewish heritage, he tells us that "form is more narrative, memory being always more narrative than the tohu-bohu of the present, which is Old Testament Hebrew, cock-sucker, for chaos and void."[45] Memory, it might be recalled, from "The Political Economy of Time," is the "mind's embodiment of form; therefore, memory, like the mind, is invariably more pure than the event. An event consists not only of forces which are opposed to one another but also forces which have no relation to the event. Whereas memory has a tendency to retain only the oppositions and the context."[46]

D. J.'s account, then, should not be taken as either full or accurate—assuming that an account possibly could be—any more than are the writings after the event in *The Armies of the Night* or *Miami and the Siege of Chicago* or Mailer's various collections of pieces. The importance of this fact to the book is that we are to mistrust the interpretation as much as the reporting of events. The parodistic phrase "purification ceremony"— a product of Tex's mind, if we are to believe D. J., after they have spontaneously set out on the trip—should not limit or even direct our reading of their motives for the trip or their activities on it. Since we cannot even be sure that the phrase occurred to Tex, we can't be sure that the boys were, at the time, actually aware of the literary analogues to their conduct. In other words, Mailer has so contrived things—notably by the speculations in nearly all of the Intro Beeps about the falsification implicit in all narrative—that the mocking lit-crit media-packaged form given to everything in D. J.'s ac-

[44] *Ibid.*, p. 74.
[45] *Ibid.*, pp. 60–61.
[46] *Cannibals and Christians*, p. 371.

celerated recollections must itself be mocked. The status
even of the parody is brought into question.

For Mailer, probably for any writer of the first rank,
questions about literary form are simultaneously questions about the shape of human consciousness. That is
why D. J.'s teasing and the joking about the authenticity
of the form of his narrative also imply that he is lying
about the past or, at the very least, that he is unable to
tell the truth, especially about his own feelings at certain moments. At one point it even seems as if D. J. is
temporarily dismissed as the narrator:

> Fuck this voice, why is D. J. hovering on the edge of
> a stall? Make your point! But D. J. is hung because
> the events now to be recounted in his private tape
> being made for the private ear of the Lord (such is
> the hypothesis now forging ahead) are hung up on a
> moment of the profoundest personal disclosure, in
> fact, dig, little punsters out in fun land, D. J. cannot
> go on because he has to talk about what Tex and him
> were presented with there all alone up above the
> Arctic Circle.[47]

Even here we can't really believe what we're being
told: the style in which we're informed that D. J. "cannot go on," like the style thereafter, is identifiably D. J.'s.
The one exception, a long passage at the end of Chap 10,
occurs over twenty pages later: the magnificent description of the scene around the pup tent just before the
two boys go to sleep, alone in the Arctic wilderness.
The feelings summoned to life in this passage might
well have belonged to D. J., and might in some diluted
form still circulate in him, but the implication is that
in telling the story two years later in Dallas he hasn't
the nerve or the style or, assuming he ever had it, a full
consciousness of those feelings. It is really only here,
and nowhere else in the book, that he is apparently

[47] *Why Are We in Vietnam?*, p. 174.

silenced—effectively enough, at least, so that the Chap which immediately follows, Chap 11, is the only one in the book without one of D. J.'s Intro Beeps. And this is the Chap in which the boys come close to a sexual joining. The surge of feeling that builds up in the passage at the end of Chap 10 and carries into Chap 11 is noticeably free of the various cants and mixed-media gags that otherwise lace every phrase in the book, even while carrying, as it must if it is to hint at existent if nearly inaccessible elements in D. J.'s consciousness, just the faintest touch of his recognizable style:

> . . . and D. J. full of iron and fire and faith was nonetheless afraid of sleep, afraid of wolves, full of beauty, afraid of sleep, full of beauty, yeah, he unashamed, for across the fire and to their side the sun was setting to the west of the pond as they looked north, setting late in the evening in remembering echo of the endless summer evening in these woods in June when darkness never came for the light never left, but it was going now, September light not fading, no, ebbing, it went in steps and starts, like going down a stair from the light to the dark, sun golden red in its purple and purple red in the black of the trees, the water was dark green and gold, a sigh came out of the night as it came on, and D. J. could have wept for a secret was near, some mystery in the secret of things —why does the odor die last and by another route?— and he knew then the meaning of trees and forest all in dominion to one another and messages across the continent on the wave of their branches up to the sorrow of the North, and great sorrow up here brought by leaves and wind some speechless electric gathering of woe, no peace in the North, not on top of the rim, and as the dark came down, a bull moose, that King Moose with antlers near to eight feet wide across all glory of spades and points, last moose of the North, came with his dewlap and his knobby knees and dumb red little eyes across the snow to lick at salt on the other side of the pond, and sunlight in the blood

of its dying[48] caught him, lit him, left him gilded red
on one side as he chomped at mud and salt, clodding
and wads dumping from his mouth to plop back in
water, like a camel foraging in a trough, deep in content, the full new moon now up before the sun was
final and down silvering the other side of this King
Moose up to the moon silhouettes of platinum on his
antlers and hide. And the water was black, and moose
dug from it and ate, and ate some more until the sun
was gone and only the moon for light and the fire of
the boys and he looked up and studied the fire some
several hundred of feet away and gave a deep caw
pulling in by some resonance of this grunt a herd of
memories of animals at work and on the march and
something gruff in the sharp wounded heart of things
bleeding somewhere in the night, a sound somewhere
in that voice in the North which spoke beneath all
else to Ranald Jethroe Jellicoe Jethroe and his friend
Gottfried (Son of Gutsy) "Texas" Hyde. They were
alone like that with the moose still staring at them.
And then the moose turned and crossed the bowl the
other way and plodded through the moonlight along
the ridges of snow, moonlight in his antlers, gloom on
his steps. And the boys slept.[49]

A cadence that is to become more and more familiar
in Mailer is beautifully at work here. It is to be found
throughout *Of a Fire on the Moon*, with its constant
telescoping of dimensions, and even more effectively in
The Armies of the Night, in the passage about heli-
copters in "A Half-Mile to Virginia," and in the fanciful
flights in "Grandma with Orange Hair," where he suggests that the poison of small-town life has been
released into the national bloodstream because "technology had driven insanity out of the wind and out of
the attic, and out of all the lost primitive places,"[50]

[48] All American editions mistakingly print "drying" for "dying."
[49] *Ibid.*, pp. 196–97.
[50] *The Armies of the Night*, p. 153.

only to concentrate it in Vegas, pro-football, suburban orgies, and, at last, Vietnam. The great achievement of the sentences in these instances, and in the passage from the novel, is that they allow the most supple possible movement back and forth between minutely observed "journalistic" details and a panorama that includes the forces that impinge upon and transform those details, perhaps to inconsequentiality. Thus the moose can be seen to have "knobby knees and dumb red little eyes," even while the "sunlight in the blood of its dying caught him, lit him, left him gilded red . . ."

The cinematic effect of this kind of writing—which can be seen sometimes in Hemingway, as in "Hills Like White Elephants," and even more frequently in Faulkner—is especially right for Mailer. Before he managed to work such sentences with the power displayed here, his need for them was already implicit in his desire to bring various styles into the closest syntactical and grammatical conjunction, especially when he wants to mix obscenities with abstractions of theory. Even more, he needed some stylistic movement that would let him find in any particular item, like Negro jazz, manifestations of a confluence of forces. In "The White Negro" the need was notably apparent as a defect in those places where he was forced to conjure up reasoned arguments —as in his claim for the possible heroism of three young hoodlums who have killed an old grocery storekeeper— where if the notion is to be promoted at all it would have to be by the power of style working to overturn rational conventions of cause and effect. And his discussion of context in the same essay, however confused, offers direct testimony that he wished consciously to blur the usual separations between an event, a participant in the event, and the context.

Each, as he sees it, is a creation of the other. The context in which a man finds himself at any given moment derives in part from the failure or success he experienced in a previous and somehow related moment. So that the context for Mailer as writer of *The Armies of the Night* was importantly affected, as we have seen, by the context of Mailer as actor, his inability as a participant in the Washington march to speak as often or as well as he would have liked. He writes as he does because he could not speak as he wanted to. Sentences of the kind being considered indicate in their very structure, that is, a writer who might have been predicted to choose, after *Why Are We in Vietnam?*, to write extraordinary spectacles. That is perhaps as good a term as any to describe *The Armies of the Night*, *Miami and the Siege of Chicago*, and *Of a Fire on the Moon*. We are invited to see him in these books within intricately related fields of force, and then to watch him act simultaneously as a participant, witness, and writer, who evokes in the clashes of his style a "war" among the various elements that constitute the life of the country and of the self. Interestingly enough, the situation of D. J. and Tex when they camp down for the night is very similar to Mailer's: they are at a place where messages are gathered from the whole continent, we are told, and where there is, at the same time, "no peace."

In these instances Mailer's style, very much in Faulknerian mode, keeps everything in motion; everything contends with, joins, is infused with everything else. Looking back at the passage just quoted, it might be said that Mailer's fondness for participles—"going," "fading," "settling," "silvering"—expresses his taste for actions that go on simultaneously, for a kind of bombardment of impressions, registered also in his repetitions of phrase, the echoings of sound, and the use of negatives which caution against fixing the picture in any familiar frame ("September light not fading, no, ebbing"). These habits, again as in Faulkner, are consistent with a tendency to collapse the rational insistence on distinctions between time and place, so that most get measured by the seasons, and between the presumably assigned functions of the senses, so that by a synesthesia of light and sound it can be suggested that the landscape sends out and receives signals. Nature, it would seem, has its own communications system without any need for technological assistance: it also has a memory that appears to work as well as a computer, made visible in the setting sun and audible in an animal grunt of the moose; it even expresses itself dialectically, as in the contending lights of the sun and moon on the two sides of the moose.

And yet if this landscape carries a message that the boys might possibly read, if its self-sufficiency frees it from human "shit" or from any kind of human genius in the form of technology, its beauty is wholly inhospitable to human love or tenderness or trust. No one could "relinquish" to it, as in Faulkner, and though the boys left their weapons behind, they wisely corrected a first impulse to leave everything and took along their bedroll, pup tent, food, matches, and binoculars. They are going into a landscape antithetical to human life, and Mailer chose to imagine it that way, rather than as anything even momentarily hospitable, like the forest in which Isaac McCaslin learned to give up his more easily disposable inheritance of "shit." In the scene that follows, the landscape induces in them a need for love, for joining together. But this need cannot ever be separated from the accompanying and equally induced desire for power and domination. Each wants to enter the other; each knows he would be killed somehow if he ever succeeded. So as they lie together, tensed in desire and fear, there was

> . . . murder between them under all friendship, for God was a beast, not a man, and God said, "Go out and kill—fulfill my will, go and kill," and they hung there each of them on the knife of the divide in all conflict of lust to own the other yet in fear of being killed by the other and as the hour went by and the lights shifted, something in the radiance of the North

went into them, and owned their fear, some communion of telepathies and new powers, and they were twins, never to be near as lovers again, but killer brothers, owned by something, prince of darkness, lord of light, they did not know.[51]

Their love for each other is a minority element already sickened by a homoerotic lust for masculine power. Such, in general, is Mailer's view of the possibilities of homosexual love, as in his writing about Genet in *The Prisoner of Sex*, where he proposes that the irony of homosexual practices is that the seemingly passive partner is really trying to take on the masculine resources of the man who enters him, and often succeeds in doing so. Homosexuality is doomed, in his view, by a contest between the partners for sexual identity which each could achieve only with a woman; they compete for what each of them has surrendered, and the sexual act ceases to have any life-giving dialectical energy.

There is scarcely any point in arguing, as some have, that the boys might have been saved for humanity if they had been able to make love. I doubt that the question is a real one here or in any of the other American novels where one finds similar male pairings. The imagination of possible destinies for friends and neighbors is a legitimate and sometimes irresistible pastime, but it is a wholly inappropriate concern when it comes to characters in a book. D. J. and Tex, Huck and Jim, for that matter, exist not to enact a life but to help realize a form; they exist in and for a structure of meaning wherein character is merely one contributory item. Mailer's maneuver at the end of the novel in fact demonstrates how the form of the book cannot be wholly surrendered to the form even of the governing consciousness within it. D. J. cannot himself express that possible saving remnant of human feeling within him which was apparently deadened at Brooks Range by

[51] *Why Are We in Vietnam?*, pp. 203–204.

the "crystallization" of his and Tex's mind. It is this same "crystallization" which in turn gives form to the narrative. We are at least allowed to wonder if D. J. and Tex possibly did have in them some thread of tangled humanity, and the pessimism of Mailer's view is most evident in the fact that when this humanity does come near to expressing itself, its only possible form is buggery—which Tex indulges in now and then anyway, just for the hell of it.

The Tenth of *The Presidential Papers*, entitled "Minorities," is given to a review of Genet's *The Blacks* which anticipates and helps explain the complex significance to *Why Are We in Vietnam?*—and also to Mailer's posture in it as a creator—of sexually perverse tensions, tensions of the kind found in Tex and D. J., in Rojack of *An American Dream*, and in Mailer himself. Buggery between two men is the equivalent in sexual conduct of D. J.'s literary conduct in the whole book. I am speaking, again, of D. J. not merely as a character, a Texas adolescent, but as a unit of energy, a composite mind, a medium for the way things are. In effect this whole book is about buggery. D. J. is merely unable to accept the clearest evidence of this in his lust for Tex, while Tex, being a sometime bugger anyway, brings this propensity into the "electrified mind" which is sealed as their common property. Recognizing this is important to an understanding of D. J.'s style, with its incessant jokes about buggery and the allusions to the North Pole as the hole of Satan. Another pair of travelers in Dante's Inferno, it might be remembered, also encounter the asshole of Satan: in the blooded arctic ices of the pit reserved for traitors. Mailer would know this, but his allusiveness in this case, interestingly enough, is never submitted to the destructive literary parody of D. J.

The book is about buggery because it is about the destruction of meaning, about that process of decreation which here, in its imagined sexual exercise, does not even alternate with acts of possible creation, as in the sexual exchanges between Rojack and Ruta in *An American Dream*. The now actively functioning connection in Mailer's imagination between sexuality, creativity—meaning writing—and the state of culture is what makes *Why Are We in Vietnam?* perhaps his most brilliant and certainly one of his central texts. It realizes in a style of fantastic comic energy a position he had articulated in *The Presidential Papers*:

> As cultures die, they are stricken with the mute implacable rage of that humanity strangled within them. So long as it grows, a civilization depends upon the elaboration of meaning, its health maintained by an awareness of its state; as it dies, a civilization opens itself to the fury of those betrayed by its meaning, precisely because that meaning was finally not sufficiently true to offer a life adequately large. The aesthetic act shifts from the creation of meaning to the destruction of it.
>
> So, one could argue, functions the therapy of the surrealist artist, of Dada, of Beat. Jaded, deadened, severed from our roots, dulled in leaden rage, inhabiting the center of the illness of the age, it becomes more excruciating each year for us to perform the civilized act of contributing to a collective meaning. The impulse to destroy moves like new air into a vacuum, and the art of the best hovers, stilled, all but paralyzed between the tension to create and the urge which is its opposite. How well Genet personifies the dilemma. Out of the tension of his flesh, he makes the pirouette of his art, offering meaning in order to adulterate it, until at the end we are in danger of being left with not much more than the narcissism of his style. How great a writer, how hideous a cage. As a civilization dies, it loses its biology. The homosexual, alienated from the biological chain, becomes its center.[52]

D. J.'s mind is an instrument for the destruction of meaning, as in the inveterate punning on names and

[52] *The Presidential Papers*, p. 210.

identities, and the adulteration of the literary, philosophical, psychological authorities to which the book alludes.
Indeed, the implication is that the form of the book,
which is also the form of D. J.'s memory, expresses the
instinctive fury of a mind which feels itself betrayed by
a civilization no longer able to sustain or elaborate in
its language any meanings which provide a life adequately humane or large. The very effort to escape that
civilization, to ventilate and cleanse the mind of its
"mixed-up shit," is betrayed both by the inhospitable
landscape to which the act, by this point in the twentieth century, has of necessity been restricted, and by the
implicit mockery of the act in the way literary analogues
to it are suggested. D. J.'s memory is doomed to scatology, and, though he dare not bugger his mate, his mind
is obsessed with jokes and images of buggery, of sexual
entrances that lead not to the centers of creations but to
the center of waste.

The book, like Mailer's comments on Genet, proposes a connection between creativity in art and in sex
that takes us to the nerve of Mailer's sense of himself as
a man and writer. "The art of the best hovers, stilled,
all but paralyzed between the tension to create and the
urge which is its opposite." It is at just such a point of
near paralysis in *Why Are We in Vietnam?* that Mailer
momentarily takes over the narrative from D. J. What
then happens is an infusion of creative vitality into an
imaginative landscape dominated by frigidities of environment and of feeling. The boys are doomed to the
kind of masculinity which has none of the dialectical
vitalities so profitably at work in Mailer: of being female
as well as male, of feeling a space within where the
gestations of imagination take place, and a keen sense
of the space without, which calls forth the will and lust
for public power. He had already written in his long
debate about scatology, "The Metaphysics of the Belly,"
that "if we wish to be more masculine we must first

satisfy something feminine in ourselves."[53] The homosexual urges of D. J. and Tex promise the reverse of this satisfaction. All they will produce is a competitive effort which will affirm the mastery of an unmodified masculinity, a narcissism of masculinity which becomes eroticized by the desire to engross the masculinity of an equally obsessed man. They are Mailerian boxers *manqué*.

For Mailer, a masculine nature that denies the minority claims within it of feminine feeling—which is how he might account for a masculinized sensibility like Kate Millett's—stiffens the imagination, prevents it from encompassing even such admission of feminine inclination, or the need of masculine support, as D. J. might have had to make in order to recall his desires for Tex. That is why Mailer, at the appropriate point, has to imagine these desires for him, and for the book, even if, as a result, the book doesn't become "crystallized." Mailer's commitment to dialectics means that he includes materials which threaten the symmetry of any possible form. His is the art of not arriving. In this case and throughout his work, dialectics is equivalent to imagination, and imagination evolves from his acceptance in himself of a feminine nature. It is probable that he associates being a writer with being a woman, and his remark in *The Prisoner of Sex* about Henry Miller and Kate Millett, even to the feminization of the males he alludes to ("dances," "curves") is a telling instance: "His work dances on the line of his dialectic. But Millett hates every evidence of the dialectic. She has a mind like a flatiron, which is to say a totally masculine mind. A hard-hat has more curves in his head."[54] If writing, creativity, a personal style distinct from an imposed one, could all be associated with femininity, then, to repeat

[53] *Ibid.*, p. 298.
[54] *The Prisoner of Sex*, p. 119.

myself, Mailer's selection of subjects, like war, boxing, politics, moonshots, and his own brawling activities, about which he writes with a boyishly self-approving apology, can be taken as counterbalancing attempts to affirm his masculinity.

In some such way it is possible to understand a central contradiction in him: there is on one hand the marvelously fastidious stylist, a writer almost precious in his care for phrasing and cadence, and, on the other and seemingly at odds, the boisterous, the vulgar actor. More often than not his style will sound like Faulkner or James, like Proust or Lawrence, even while he is pushing Papa Hemingway as a model and precursor. As recently as *Cannibals and Christians* he misreads Lawrence out of what I would guess is an anxiety to appear tougher than he really is, which means that Lawrence must be made less so. Lawrence, he there claims, is so sentimental about lovers that he misses their desire to "destroy one another; lovers change one another; lovers resist the change that each gives to the other."[55]

This is of course not what Lawrence misses. It is what he insists on. Not Lawrence but Mailer is deficient in imagining such relationships between a man and a woman. When the sexes meet in Mailer's novels it is either for frantic sexual experiences or for conferences about manners and role-playing that never significantly modify either one. When he tries to get beyond this, as in *An American Dream*, he surrounds the relationship with portents and circumstances that prevent it from ever becoming more than an alliance for some mutual escape to an imagined ordinariness never to be achieved. Perhaps the reason for this is that the conflicts that might bring about a change in the relationships between men and women actually take place only *within* the nature of all the men in his works, within his own nature. Mailer is finally the most androgynous of writ-

55 *Cannibals and Christians*, p. 198.

ers. Perhaps that is why, of what are now nineteen books, only five are novels, a form where some developed relationship between the sexes is generally called for, and the rest (except for a quite good volume of poems entitled *Deaths for the Ladies (and Other Disasters)* and the scripts for his play *The Deer Park* and his film *Maidstone*) is a species of self-reporting.

Yet for all the self-reporting what do we know about him? Very little. Next to nothing about his childhood, his schooling; very little about his love affairs, not much more about his friends or his wives. Though there are bits of incidental intelligence about drinking and drugs in *Advertisements for Myself* and about his fourth marriage in *The Armies of the Night* and *Of a Fire on the Moon*, and though we learn in *The Prisoner of Sex* that for part of one summer he kept house for six children before an old love, who was to become the mother of a seventh, arrived to rescue him, most of what we get from this presumably self-centered, egotistic, and self-revealing writer are anecdotes about his public performances. Even these prove to be not confessions so much as self-creations after the event, presentations of a self he makes up for his own as much as for the reader's inspection.

This is not said critically but rather to suggest that Mailer's genius is excited by those very elements in him and in the nation which prevent the solidification of either one. Solidification, or what D. J. calls "crystallization," is not the function of Mailer's art and is instead ascribed to those forces in contemporary civilization to which his art opposes itself. With what seems at times obtuseness, he chooses to put his stress of appreciation on those aspects of a subject which anyone working in the rationalist, humanist, liberal tradition would generally choose to ignore or condemn. He is, therefore, necessarily committed to the democratic principle that all parts of any subject are at least initially equal. Like Glenn Gould playing Bach or Beethoven, Mailer decides that what everyone else treats as a subordinate sound can be treated as a major one. This significantly complicates the responses called forth by some of the characters in his later work. Thus, while D. J. and Tex are agents of some horrid, proliferating power that propels America into Vietnam, they are also in another sense "good." They are emphatically and unapologetically what they are; they do what they do well, and it is possible in Mailer to do anything well, to perform well even in the act of murder.

For that reason the obscenity in *Why Are We in Vietnam?* is not a symptom of what is the matter with D. J. Instead, it is a clue to what might possibly be "good" about him. In "An Evening with Jackie Kennedy, or, the Wild West of the East," Mailer proposed to tell her "that the obscene had a right to exist in the novel," a desire typical of his wish to bring apparently uncongenial ideas into situations designed to exclude them. As "queen of the arts" she would understand, he likes to think, that it was "the purpose of culture finally to enrich all the psyche, not just part of us" because "Art in all its manifestations . . . including the rude, the obscene, and the unsayable . . . was as essential to the nation as technology."[56] Elsewhere he makes the point that an artist who does not bring into art those qualities which might disrupt formal coherence is guilty of doing to art, and to culture, what Eisenhower did to politics during what were for Mailer the worst years of his time in America: "He did not divide the nation as a hero might (with a dramatic dialogue as a result); he merely excluded one part of the nation from the other. The result was an alienation of the best minds and bravest impulses from the faltering history which was made."[57]

Mailer will exclude nothing in the interests of formal

56 *The Presidential Papers*, p. 92.
57 *Ibid.*, p. 43.

arrangements. This has led to the most consistent misunderstanding of his work: the failure to grasp why he is given to obscenity and violence. In "An Impolite Interview" with Paul Krassner of *The Realist*, he makes his position on these matters clear enough, but in such a way as perhaps only further to confuse his detractors. Alluding to an Italian bombardier who reported that the bombs bursting over an Ethiopian village were beautiful, he writes that while he does not necessarily disapprove of violence in a man or a woman, "what I still disapprove of is *inhuman* violence," which is of course the kind infused into D. J. and Tex at Brooks Range.

> I disapprove of bombing a city. I disapprove of the kind of man who will derive aesthetic satisfaction from the fact that an Ethiopian village looks like a red rose at the moment the bombs are exploding. I won't disapprove of the act of perception which witnesses that: I think that act of perception is—I'm going to use the word again—noble.
>
> What I'm getting at is: a native village is bombed, and the bombs happen to be beautiful when they land; in fact it would be odd if all that sudden destruction did not liberate some beauty. The form a bomb takes in its explosion may be in part a picture of the potentialities it destroyed. So let us accept the idea that the bomb is beautiful.
>
> If so, any liberal who decries the act of bombing is totalitarian if he doesn't admit as well that the bombs were indeed beautiful.
>
> Because the moment we tell something that's untrue, it does not matter how pure our motives may be—the moment we start mothering mankind and decide that one truth is good for them to hear and another is not so good, because while we can understand, those poor ignorant unfortunates cannot—then what are we doing, we're depriving the minds of others of knowledge which may be essential.
>
> Think of a young pilot who comes along later, some young pilot who goes out on a mission and isn't prepared for the fact that a bombing might be beautiful;

he could conceivably be an idealist, there were some in the war against Fascism. If the pilot is totally unprepared he might never get over the fact that he was particularly thrilled by the beauty of that bomb.

But if our culture had been large enough to say that Ciano's son-in-law not only found that bomb beautiful, but that indeed this act of perception was *not* what was wrong; the evil was to think that this beauty was worth the lot of living helpless people who were wiped out broadside. Obviously whenever there's destruction, there's going to be beauty implicit in it.[58]

Truth for Mailer is equivalent to the acceptance, with respect to any subject, of such a range of diverse feelings that some seem to cancel or mutilate the others, and there are times when his commitment to truth cannot escape a perverse exaltation of the submerged at the expense of the humanly self-evident. While he is clearly aware of this danger, he will not allow the presumed exigencies of the humanly self-evident, much less the exigencies of literary form or of logic, to dictate what he puts in or leaves out. This is what distinguishes him from his contemporaries in fiction. However different, they all find it necessary at some point to suppress what I have called the minority within: those feelings, expressions, possibilities in the material that are perhaps incommensurate with the effect being striven for. Mailer's honesty in this is rather more strenuous and altogether more expensive than theirs.

Unfortunately, the most noble of instincts have a way of being transformed first into self-consciousness, then into habit, and finally into mechanics. What was once a virtue becomes a tic; what was once romantic becomes, as Byron discovered, burlesque. Even in this passage, and increasingly to the detriment of his work, Mailer often creates divisions in his material so simplistically extreme as to allow him an unearned rest, exonerated, in the middle of it all, freed of choice or even tempta-

[58] *Ibid.*, pp. 136–37.

tion. Positioned between extremities which he has himself invented and which are by no means made necessary
by the nature of what he is trying to account for, he
reveals at times "some wistful desire to be less extraordinary," a desire attributed to Deirdre in *An American
Dream*.[59] Being among the most self-scrutinizing of
writers and his own best critic, he has come even to
wonder in *The Prisoner of Sex* "if his vision, for lack of
some cultivation in the middle, was not too compul-
sively ready for the apocalyptic."[60] "Cultivation" is the
important clue here; he thinks of the middle as a place
where his imagination does not instinctively move and
where it becomes flabby. *Miami and the Siege of
Chicago* and *Of a Fire on the Moon* are the clearest
instances, and it is significant that both involved him in
events in which for various reasons he could not directly
participate. In the one his deadline for the book pre-
vented him from acting in any way that might get him
arrested, as he was in the Washington of *The Armies of
the Night*; in the other, the very nature of technological
enterprise excluded from participation anyone not
expertly tooled into it. An unwonted self-pity has
become the sign of such moments ("no revolution had
arisen in the years when he was ready—the timing of his
soul was apocalyptically maladroit,"[61] he tells us while
watching the Yippies from the nineteenth floor of his
hotel), along with a hectoring, envious tone with respect
to persons, and a stylistic failure to engage himself except through easy hyperbole. Are we really to think that
the vibration of Yippie music in Lincoln Park "was the
road of the beast in all nihilism,"[62] or rather that the
sound reminded Mailer that his own voice simply could
not be accommodated to it?

Despite some stunning exceptions, like the last chap-

[59] *An American Dream*, p. 214.
[60] *The Prisoner of Sex*, p. 204.
[61] *Miami and the Siege of Chicago*, p. 188.
[62] *Ibid.*, p. 142.

ter, "A Burial by the Sea," in *Of a Fire on the Moon*, there is evidence that Mailer's imagination of himself is becoming dangerously rigid and circumscribed, particularly when he indulges in rather simple and fashionable concerns about the future of the imagination in an age of science and technology. Where before there was a supple, intimate, and daring search within his schematizations for pressures that would unsettle them, the tendency now is to insist that the events or persons he writes about should fit the scheme. His most impressive writing at the moment seems to occur where he is least ambitious. The best parts of *Of a Fire on the Moon*, for example, are the descriptive ones; the most aggravating are the efforts to sort out what he is describing so that his hyperbolic rhetoric can go to work.

Perhaps his strength at the moment derives more from what he is learning to do by making movies than from what he has already learned by making dualisms. *Of a Fire on the Moon* reveals his genius, so evident in his political writing, for quick characterizations of a kind not tied to any dialectical issue (Frank McGee is said to have a "personality all reminiscent . . . of a coach of a rifle team"), for casual but packed analogies that Lowell might envy ("what if the moon were as quiet as the fisherman when he lays the fly on the water"), for Proustian social observations (as in the account of an evening at the Houston home of European friends). And he is sometimes even closer to Lawrence than he was before in his capacity for imaginative drifts and extensions, all the while being moved forward by what seem to be the accidental associations of language. Not in his by now mechanical intellectual superstructurings but in these more open evidences of his power there is assurance enough that technology has not yet collapsed the language or stilled the imagination. His superlative description of the cratered face of the moon is the product of intense research—it should be added that Mailer is, by the way, a first-rate scholar—and it excels anything made available in words or pictures by the machined men of the Apollo flights.

The book is made heavy by ambitions in excess of what is brilliantly accomplished. Too much of it is put on loan to one of the now overfamiliar dualisms: technology and intuition, the Sanitary-Lobe and the Wild-Lobe nesting together in every American, technological reality and the reality of death, Von Braun as a man of opposites, NASA as having in it the sound of Nazi even though technology and Nazism may be inimical to one another, the space program as insane or noble, "a search for the good, or the agent of diabolisms yet unglimpsed."[63] The book is continually caught up in these dualisms in a nearly manic way—as if otherwise it might fall to pieces. Faced with the clear evidence that the astronauts, differences among them waived, are by nature rather flat-minded fellows, Mailer is momentarily bewildered. What to do with material so unyielding, so uniform? This is rather a new problem for him, but all he can produce are old questions and their answers. He proceeds, as is his wont, to divide in order to conquer. Divide the material, argue the differences, reach a kind of stalemate, and call it a "mystery."

It is by such means that the book engages itself with the subject of dreams. After all, the only life other than the irredeemably evident one that Mailer can propose for men of such rectitude has to be in the unconscious. He can thereby give them a double life. However spurious it might be, it lets him speculate that to dwell "in the very center of technological reality . . . yet to inhabit . . . if only in one's dreams—that other world where death, metaphysics and the unanswerable questions of eternity must reside, was to suggest natures so divided that they could have been the most miserable and unbalanced of men if they did not contain in their huge

[63] *Of a Fire on the Moon*, p. 140.

contradictions some of the profound and accelerating opposites of the century itself."[64]

Having decided to create a division in the astronauts by populating their unconscious, Mailer can then only become increasingly hyperbolic about them; their unconscious cannot be individuated; it must instead contain the historical, metaphysical, and social components he needs for the swelling rhetoric of his book. He cannot be expected to allow their dreams to be the result of anything so merely personal as sublimation. Nor would he, having escalated his terms to this point, settle for the idea that the voyage represents merely a larger, corporate effort at the sublimation "of aggressive and intolerably inhuman desires."[65] Even as he allows that possibility, he prefers to divide the matter more ostentatiously: the astronauts and their flight may be the instruments of "celestial or satanic endeavors."[66] We are back again to God and the Devil.

Why, it has to be asked, must he persist in these by now deadening acts of cosmic division? Their function is best understood, and made less debilitating, I suspect, if they are taken less as part of the substance of the moon book than as its necessary fuel, its lubricant even. They are what he needs now to get himself moving, get himself involved and boosted to a level of intensity where he will then be able to produce the masterful straight stuff, like his description of the Vehicle Assembly Building at Cape Kennedy. He even admits to the opportunistic side of his practices; "It was somehow superior,"[67] he explains, to think of the flight in cosmic rather than in less exalting terms, and when he wants to claim that the trip might "reveal some secret in the buried tendencies of our history," he has to agree in the next paragraph that "such remarks are large, they

[64] *Ibid.*, p. 47.
[65] *Ibid.*, p. 152.
[66] *Loc. cit.*
[67] *Loc. cit.*

are grand, they roll off into the murk of metaphysical storm."[68] Mailer's own anxieties of late are most evident in the frequency of such near disclaimers, near apologies for his own inflations.

There is of course nothing necessarily the matter with inflations or even with the excuse, however sophomoric, that by indulging in them Mailer is showing what it is like to take a space trip in the mind. And few would object to what Mailer at one point proposes as the justification for the scale of his enterprise: "a first reconnaissance into the possibility of restoring magic, psyche, and the spirits of the underworld to the spookiest venture in history, a landing on the moon, an event whose technologese had been so complete that the word 'spook' probably did not appear in twenty million words of NASA prose."[69] It is simply that in this book Mailer proves less a Prospero of *The Tempest* than a Glendower of *Henry IV*, though a Glendower shrewd enough to anticipate the riposte to his claim that he "can call spirits from the vasty deep": "Why so can I, or so can any man;/But will they come when you do call for them?"

I suppose it could be said that the book is meant to demonstrate why there will never be now in America the revolution feared in *The Armies of the Night*. The Wasps have won by default, those "Faustian, barbaric, draconian, progress-oriented, and root-destroying people."[70] They are coming into control of evolution, and the literary imagination, with all the odors and obscenities that nourish it, is at last obsolete, with this book proposing itself as one of the final records, as Christopher Lehmann-Haupt has suggested. The last chapter almost says as much. More likely Mailer's standard routines have simply become obsolete. I think they probably have. Besides, the points where he is not doing

[68] *Ibid.*, p. 161.
[69] *Ibid.*, p. 131.
[70] *The Armies of the Night*, p. 10.

his routines show that he still can, in his own phrase, "climb to capture the language again."[71]

Now at a crisis in his writing equivalent, I suspect, to the early period of exhaustion after *The Deer Park*, Mailer is uniquely situated to escape the entrapment that often turns American writers into imitators and, finally, into unconscious parodists of themselves. His situation is unique because some of his most brilliant work is literary self-criticism. In *The Prisoner of Sex* there are already hints of a healthy negative assessment of where he is, of boredom with characteristic and familiar ways of doing things. Finally, he is even at "war" with his own achievements, and out of this may emerge still other, different forms for himself, for contemporary life, and for our language.

[71] *Ibid.*, p. 56.

SHORT BIBLIOGRAPHY

INDEX

SHORT BIBLIOGRAPHY

"A Checklist of Mailer's Published Work" from 1941 to 1970 can be found in Robert F. Lucid, ed. *Norman Mailer: The Man and His Work*, Boston, 1971.

BOOKS BY MAILER

The Naked and the Dead. New York: Rinehart, 1948. Novel.
Barbary Shore. New York: Rinehart, 1951. Novel.
The Deer Park. New York: Putnam's, 1955. Novel.
Advertisements for Myself. New York: Putnam's, 1959. Miscellany.
Deaths for the Ladies (and Other Disasters). New York: Putnam's, 1962. Poems.
The Presidential Papers. New York: Putnam's, 1963. Miscellany.
An American Dream. Monthly installments appeared in *Esquire*, January–August, 1964. Published, after revision, in book form by The Dial Press, 1965. Novel.
Cannibals and Christians. New York: The Dial Press, 1966. Miscellany.

The Deer Park, a Play. New York: The Dial Press, 1967. Play, with introduction by the author.

The Short Fiction of Norman Mailer. New York: Dell, 1967. Paperback collection, with an introduction by the author.

Why Are We in Vietnam? New York: Putnam's, 1967. Novel.

The Idol and the Octopus: Political Writings of Norman Mailer on the Kennedy and Johnson Administrations. New York: Dell, 1968. Paperback collection, with an introduction by the author.

The Armies of the Night. New York: New American Library, 1968. Narrative-journal.

Miami and the Siege of Chicago. New York: New American Library, 1968. Narrative-journal.

Of a Fire on the Moon. Boston: Little, Brown, 1970. Narrative-journal.

The Prisoner of Sex. Boston: Little, Brown, 1971. Speculations.

On the Fight of the Century: "King of the Hill." New York: Signet paperback, 1971. On the Muhammad Ali–Joe Frazier fight for the heavyweight championship of the world, with illustrations.

Maidstone: A Mystery. New York: New American Library, 1971. Paperback edition of the film script with an introduction by the author, "A Course in Film-Making," first published in *New American Review*, number 12.

Existential Errands. Boston: Little, Brown, 1972. Miscellany.

WRITINGS ABOUT MAILER

A. In books:

Aldridge, John. *After the Lost Generation.* New York: McGraw-Hill, 1951.

Baldwin, James. *Nobody Knows My Name.* New York: The Dial Press, 1962.

Flaherty, Joe. *Managing Mailer.* New York: Coward-McCann, 1970.

Foster, Richard. *Norman Mailer.* Minneapolis: University of Minnesota Pamphlets on American Writers, No. 73, 1968.

Gilman, Richard. *The Confusion of Realms.* New York: Random House, 1969.

Guttmann, Allen. *The Jewish Writers in America.* New York, 1971.

Hassan, Ihab. *Radical Innocence.* Princeton, New Jersey: Princeton University Press, 1961.

Howe, Irving. *A World More Attractive.* New York: Horizon Press, 1963.

Kaufmann, Donald L. *Norman Mailer: The Countdown (The First Twenty Years).* Carbondale: Southern Illinois University Press, 1969. (Included is a useful bibliography of critical studies of Mailer up to 1966.)

Kazin, Alfred. *Contemporaries.* Boston: The Atlantic Monthly Press, 1962.

Langbaum, Robert. *The Modern Spirit.* New York: Oxford University Press, 1970.

Lasch, Christopher. *The New Radicalism in America, 1889–1963.* New York: Knopf, 1965.

Leeds, Barry H. *The Structural Vision of Norman Mailer.* New York: New York University Press, 1969.

Lucid, Robert F., ed. *Norman Mailer: The Man and His Work.* Boston: Little, Brown, 1971. Previously published essays by seventeen critics, with an introduction by the editor.

Ludwig, Jack. *Recent American Novelists.* Minneapolis: University of Minnesota Press, 1962.

Manso, Peter, ed. *Running Against the Machine.* New York: Doubleday, 1969. Impressions and position papers by various writers having to do with Mailer's primary campaign in 1969 for nomination as Mayor of New York.

Podhoretz, Norman. *Doings and Undoings.* New York: Farrar, Straus, 1964.

Sheed, Wilfred. *The Morning After.* New York: Farrar, Straus and Giroux, 1971.

Tanner, Tony. *The City of Words: American Fiction, 1950–1970.* New York: Harper and Row, 1971.

Vidal, Gore. *Rocking the Boat.* Boston: Little, Brown, 1962.

B. *In periodicals:*

Bersani, Leo. "The Interpretation of Dreams," *Partisan Review* (fall 1965). Reprinted in Lucid, ed., *Norman Mailer: The Man and His Work.*

Bone, Robert. "Private Mailer Re-enlists," *Dissent* (autumn 1960).

Brooks, Peter. "The Melodramatic Imagination." *Partisan Review* (No. 2, 1972).

Carroll, Paul. *Playboy* Interview, *Playboy* (January 1968). Reprinted in the Lucid collection.

DeMott, Benjamin. "Docket No. 15833," *American Scholar* (spring 1961).

Goldman, Laurence. "The Political Vision of Norman Mailer," *Studies on the Left* (summer 1964).

Hampshire, Stuart. "Mailer United," *New Statesman* (October 13, 1961).

Kermode, Frank. "Rammel," *New Statesman* (May 14, 1965).

MacDonald, Dwight. "Art, Life and Violence," *Commentary* (June 1962).

Martien, Norman. "Norman Mailer at Graduate School," *New American Review*, I (September 1967). Reprinted in the Lucid collection.

Modern Fiction Studies, XVII, No. 3, autumn 1971. This issue is devoted to essays on Mailer and provides a checklist of critical studies up to 1971.

Richardson, Jack. "The Aesthetics of Norman Mailer," *The New York Review of Books* (May 8, 1969). Reprinted in the Lucid collection.

Richler, Mordecai. "Norman Mailer," *Encounter* (July 1965).

Rosenbaum, Ron. "The Siege of Mailer: Hero to Historian," *The Village Voice*, January 21, 1971.

Toback, James. "Norman Mailer Today," *Commentary* (October 1967).

Trilling, Diana. "Norman Mailer," *Encounter* (November 1962). Reprinted in the Lucid collection, entitled "The Moral Radicalism of Norman Mailer."

INDEX